FINDING THE MEANING OF GRIEF

6 WEEKS OF DEVOTIONALS FOR EXPLORING COMFORT & HOPE

JANET HANEY

Copyright © 2024 by Janet Haney

All rights reserved.

Cover design by Emily Ann Peterson; "Flowers" by JRyde; adapted and licensed under CC by 2.0.

No part of this book may be reproduced in any form or by any electronic or mechanical means, including information storage and retrieval systems, without written permission from the author, except for the use of brief quotations in a book review.

This book may be purchased in bulk for promotional, educational, or business use. Please contact Janet and her team at jhaney.com

ISBN 978-0-9997294-4-1 (ebook)

ISBN 978-0-9997294-3-4 (paperback)

First Edition: 2024

I share my story and dedicate this book to you, so you can find your own meaning of grief and have the courage to share your journey.

CONTENTS

Introduction	ix

WEEK ONE: FINDING MEANING IN EMPTY PLACES

1. Roots by the Stream	3
2. Connecting with Solitude	7
3. Anger Hacks	10
4. Dancing with Disappointment	14
5. Punching Down on Pain	17
6. Loss Before the Loss	21
7. New Parking Spots (Recipe: Mom's Sweet Tea)	24

WEEK TWO: FINDING MEANING IN CHANGE

8. Rearranging Furniture & Unwanted Change	31
9. Deep Waters of Preparation	36
10. Comparing Apples to Lasagna	41
11. Nurturing Joy with Newness	46
12. Reordering Space & Relationships	50
13. Downsizing & Donation Boxes	55
14. A New Familiar (Recipe: Potato Chip Grilled Cheese)	58

WEEK THREE: FINDING MEANING IN YOUR JOURNEY

15. Sinking Sand	67
16. Finding the Solid Ground	72
17. The Solo Pilgrimage	76
18. Rebuilding & Learning to Accept	79
19. The Sun Also Rises	83
20. Lifting Your Eyes	86
21. Finding Stability After Change (Recipe: Dijon Mustard Salad Dressing)	90

WEEK FOUR: FINDING MEANING IN A NEW PATH

22. Taking Exits & New Opportunities	97
23. Lace Up the Shoes	103
24. Rest for Restoration	107
25. Sweet Meditations (Recipe: Caramel)	111
26. A New Way Within	116
27. Counting Doors	121
28. Flavor Profiles of Grief (Recipe: Herb Sprinkled Popcorn)	125

WEEK FIVE: FINDING MEANING IN RESTORATION

29. Renewed Strength	133
30. Catching Curveballs	138
31. Navigating A New Boat	143
32. Relaxing into Your Worries	147
33. Suffering & Enduring	152
34. One Balloon at a Time	159
35. Comfort in Clarity (Recipe: Comfort Creamy Potato Soup)	164

WEEK SIX: FINDING MEANING IN REMEMBERING

36. Celebrating Within Grief	171
37. Reminisce	176
38. Memory Lane	181
39. Celebrating Milestones	187
40. Letting Go of Stubborn Anger	192
41. Sufficient Grace	197
42. Telling Your Story	201

APPENDIX

Group Guide for Finding The Meaning of Grief	209
More Tools & Activities	211
More Writing Prompts	214
More Scriptures for Hope	220

RECOMMENDED READING

Shameless Plugs	229
Grief & Faith	231
Books That Encourage Journaling	236

Non-Fiction   239
Devotionals   242
Grief Books for Kids   244

MORE RECIPES
Homemade Applesauce   251
Baked Apples   253
Really Easy Tomato Soup   255
Carol's Whack-Biscuit Chicken Casserole   257
Cathy's Stuffed Mushrooms   259
Super Easy Pot Pie   261
Super Meatloaf   263
Lori's Angel Hair Spaghetti Pie   265
Jeanette's Fabulous Frosted Brownies   267
Fresh Strawberry Cream Pie   269
Better Than Store Bought Chocolate Sauce   271
Crock Pot Pork Chops   273
Slow Cooker Pulled Pork   275
Super Good BBQ Sauce   277
Slaw   278
Prosciutto Wrapped Asparagus   280
Chris's Fresh Salmon Three Ways   282

Acknowledgments   285
About the Author   287
Also by Janet Haney   289

INTRODUCTION

"And call upon me in the day of trouble; I will deliver you, and you will honor me."

Psalm 50:15

No one knows what your grief truly feels like except you. Yet grief is a universal experience.

Grief is real. It's easy for grief to rear its head in anger, depression, or irritability. It demands our recognition and honesty.

Grief hurts. The pain is real and physical. It can be crushing. It can manifest itself in the most unexpected ways and at the most unexpected times. Yet there is the expected pain, too. In the early days, I changed my daily routine to avoid the pangs of grief attached to things like seeing school buses or driving by certain buildings. For many of us, our pain is riveting and profound.

Grief is isolating, no matter the cause of the heartache or how many people surround you. It's easy to pull inside yourself and not want to

INTRODUCTION

come out. Grief is uncharted waters, a place to disorient and lose your way quickly.

Grief isn't just tied up in death. It shows up with loss or heartbreak of all kinds. When a job is lost, a friend abandons, a relationship is betrayed, cancer is diagnosed, a car accident takes its toll—grief breaks into the window of our soul.

Grief is rarely discussed, but we've all had it knock on the door for some reason.

Grief brings struggle. These happened on the most challenging days of my losses. Small attempts to read anything felt like a miracle, especially if the topic concerned loss, widowhood, grief, or grieving. The worst days of struggle made it too difficult even to read a bereavement card. I'd open the envelope to make a note of the sender, put the card back inside, and toss it in a box.

Grief has a way of taking the color out of life, often our soul, and especially bereavement cards. It wasn't that I didn't appreciate the care and concern intended by each sender—I was touched by this, truly.

Grief can bring exhaustion. I feared that even hearing about someone else's grief over a shared loss would be too big a burden for my already unbearable and heavy losses. Reading about grief or learning about the grieving process was too much to ask on those days.

Grief has a knack for collecting grief books. I managed to acquire stacks and stacks of pages on the subject. Despite this, on many of my darkest grief days, I lacked the strength for heavy-handed how-to grief guides; I could barely lift myself out of bed. The last thing I needed was an additional stack to my heavy, overwhelming to-do lists.

So, if you're hesitant to pick up this or any other grief-related book, I *certainly* understand. I've been in a similar place.

WHY I WROTE *FINDING THE MEANING OF GRIEF*

Instead, I needed empathy, an empty page to write on, and an easy prompt with permission to spend as little as 5 minutes, especially

INTRODUCTION

when that was all I could manage. I needed someone else who understood the same pang of guilt during a rare bright spot. I needed nudges to take things one day at a time and reminders to cherish the many ways time continues to pass.

***Finding the Meaning of Grief* exists because we all grieve differently and for many different reasons.** Lest there is any confusion, your meaning of grief is *yours* to define.

This is the grief journey I have walked so many times. I pray this book can be a source of comfort to ease your travel through a grieving season.

I've learned through my many losses that nothing makes sense of grief unless we allow it to change us for the better. However, this change is a journey that requires courage and faith to look straight into the dark tunnel of it. Faith and knowing God's love are the tools needed to believe that loss and grief experienced in life have a purpose and courage even when nothing makes sense.

***Finding the Meaning of Grief* is the devotional book I wish I had.** When I was in similar shoes to yours, I wish I had something like this to come alongside to offer understanding and empathy while gently encouraging me to learn *through* my grief. This book is just that: small, daily "recipes" you can try out when you need an extra dose of softness, space, comfort food, or permission to grieve how you need to grieve on that particular day. Take them, try them, or leave them as is.

Consider this book a place to sit for a few minutes, spend time with someone who understands grief, and consider a specific action or activity.

This book encourages survival on those hardest days, no matter how deep your wound is. Healing comes often in unexpected ways and at its own pace. If you are open to it, grief transforms us and can teach us lessons that come only from a crucible of pain.

Life settles in around our losses. Nothing is the same, but the key is to let yourself adapt to the new normal. It's not better, just new. We learn to live around the hole left by the missing piece of life, and that's a choice. How we react is our only point of control when dealing with loss. Anger, sadness, feeling blank inside, and depression are all normal. Tears are normal, too. Let them flow, no matter when they decide to show up.

I made it a habit always to carry a handkerchief wherever I went. It was much more substantial than a tissue and could withstand getting crushed in my fist. Holding onto something, like a handkerchief or a scripture, when those heart-stab memories burst through your heart helps. The Lord is close to the broken-hearted, even if His breath feels too soft to detect. God wants to travel the path next to you.

"The LORD is close to the broken-hearted; He rescues those who are crushed in spirit."

Psalm 34:18 NLT

MY STORY, THE SHORT-VERSION

My journey with grief is uniquely mine, and yours is uniquely yours. When pain touches pain, there is an understanding that needs few words. As such, you'll hear bits and pieces of my story throughout this book. Before continuing, it might feel helpful to get acquainted with the "headline version" of my grief journey:

- Many years ago, my 9-year-old boy woke up in heaven after suffering an out-of-the-blue seizure during his sleep.
- Later, my husband fought cancer for 11 years. Eventually, an inoperable cancer took him at age 58 to be with our son.
- After heroically enduring these tragedies, my brilliant daughter walked through the doors of destiny to begin life on her own. I learned how to support her long distance from a very empty nest.
- Then breast cancer struck my own life, and I walked that health journey as a widow.

INTRODUCTION

Note: The detailed versions of these stories are written in my memoir *Hello Nobody Standing At the Door Alone What to Do When Everything Changes.*

If it were up to me to write the recipe of a person's life, the above stories would never be included as ingredients at all. The meaning of my grief is similar to a batter made in the kitchen. Each heartache cracked and poured into the bowl. Once each ingredient of loss stirred into my life, the batter was changed, too.

If you're reading this book, you might already understand this more than you ever wished. You may be many years into your exploration to find the meaning of grief.

Everyone sits at the table of heartbreak, eventually.

WHAT THIS BOOK IS FOR

On your deepest, darkest days, *Finding the Meaning of Grief* can provide you the words of encouragement I wish I had while going through my hardest days. I needed someone to come alongside me, tell me to "keep going," and feel the grief one day or one small minute at a time.

On the days when you wish you had someone to talk to about grief, *Finding the Meaning of Grief* can provide an outlet when others in your life might not know how to talk about it. Many don't know how to find the ways that comfort and grief can co-exist.

On the days when you're asking, "What next?" I've been lost in the woods of heartache and left asking, "What am I supposed to do now?" While this book is not an outright "how-to," it *can* help by providing some activities to sort through your loss and confusion. I can point you in the direction I took, but the path forward is yours to take.

On the days when you're ready to take a deep breath, roll up your sleeves, and process some grief, this can be a book to help you dig deeper into that journey.

On days when you've already processed too much grief and wish to

INTRODUCTION

rest, *Finding the Meaning of Grief* can help you take a step back without stepping back from everything in life.

WHAT'S INSIDE THIS BOOK?

This book provides daily, flexible, optional actions and a creative perspective for your unique circumstance. I've done this in multiple ways, outlined below.

Daily Reading

The structure of daily devotionals reflects a recipe's framework for our spiritual life. Plus, devotionals can be a helpful tool for the grieving process. Daily nudges are helpful reminders that the Lord is in this season along with you.

Quotes & Scripture

In each day's reading, you'll find quotes that I've found comforting, inspiring, and encouraging. I've also included many scriptures throughout.

I have found that God is a significant ingredient in my grieving process. He is what makes all components bind together in purpose and fulfillment. He can be your comfort in empty places, as he was mine. He can give meaning to a meaningless circumstance.

My faith and personal relationship with Jesus is what carried me through the darkest days of my grief and has given me a peace inside I could never give myself, no matter how much I tried. On the most unsteady days, He smooths out the road before me. He can do that for you, too.

Daily Activity

Grief is more than reading a book about it. It must be lived and done with action and full-in-body. In this spirit, each day's reading includes daily activities.

These are optional opportunities to explore further, so I've placed each under the Try This label. Do these activities any day, any time you feel

INTRODUCTION

like it (or don't feel like it, but know it might be good for you to try it out gently.)

For variety, you'll find a mix of Scripture to ponder, journal prompts to try, or assignments to make a connection. On other days, you might find a suggestion, helpful lists to make, a creative exercise, or some physical movement.

Back-of-the-Book Bonuses

In the back of the book, you'll find additional prompts that might inspire more journal writing. There's also a list of some of my favorite scriptures to consider and a few more creative activities to try.

Recommended Reading

I've included a list and a summary of some of the books I have on my shelf that I've found helpful. This includes books on grief, other devotionals, and even grief books I recommend to share with children.

Group Discussion Guide

I've included a versatile group discussion guide in the Appendices for those who want to work through this book in a group. You may get a few ideas for a grief group of your own. A group can be as small as yourself and another person or be a more formal setting sponsored by your church or community group. Discuss the daily readings and journal prompts, or pick an activity to do together. There are many ways to make the format of this book fit your needs.

Weekly Recipes

Finally, each week includes an easy, simple, and yummy recipe you can try out in the kitchen. The chosen recipes are favorites from my kitchen, extended family, and personal go-to's I've found comforting.

Additional favorite recipes are at the back of the book under More Recipes. Give them a try; nothing says comfort more than sitting down to share food with someone you care about.

Why Recipes?

INTRODUCTION

Times of grief and casserole drop-offs go hand in hand. I remember how packed our refrigerator was with many lasagnas and just as many chicken and rice casseroles. I appreciated the well-wishers' kindness in bringing food to the house, but it was a long time after the funeral before we could eat casseroles again.

All that to say, grief and food go hand in hand. Often, it's the only way someone can express how they care.

Recipe reading is a pastime of mine. I have stacks and stacks of cooking magazines all over my house, including notebooks filled with recipes printed from the internet. My love of cooking and entertaining sent me to culinary school, which opened my eyes to the complexity and beauty of good food. This experience helped me realize how important a good recipe is. This is true in cooking and life.

Food is a 1) comfort and a 2) central point for community. We need both food and community to endure our grief.

MY PRAYER FOR YOU

Grief isn't fair. It has a way of finding us. Heartbreak, disappointment, divorce, illness, an accident, loss of a job, or an empty nest: the list of grief-makers goes on and on. The only control over our losses is how we allow them to reframe us.

This book, *Finding the Meaning of Grief*, is a small way to introduce encouragement for the path on which you find yourself. I wish I could come and sit beside you in your season of grief, with an arm around your shoulder to say, "You can do this," because you can. I know you can because I did it, and I did it more than once.

I hope *Finding the Meaning of Grief* will be a companion to your grief. No one has the exact formula to make your heartache go away, but it does help to know you aren't alone. I've been there, and so have many others.

No matter where they come from, our losses mark us in unique ways. No one else can walk your steps of grief, tell you how to do it, or point

INTRODUCTION

to its purpose for you. These are for you to discover with each minute, each day, each month lived with grief.

I've known others who showed their grief much differently than frequent or even infrequent gravesite visits. Other people are not grieving the loss of a person at all. We grieve through the loss of jobs, relationships, unfulfilled dreams, or failing health. We grieve when kids leave home, when animals die, or when houses are torn down.

Some folks seek out comfort as the dust settles. Others want to move on as fast as possible, while others need time to get familiar with the new pain of grief before seeking out comfort.

There are people ahead of you who have traveled these roads longer and survived the dark and dry seasons of their grief. Still, others have just tied on the boots required to endure life with what's ahead. No matter the spot you find yourself, there's a community in knowing we, the grievers, get it. We've been there and know what it feels like.

You'll Know When You're Ready

You might need more time to be ready for this book. It's here whenever you need it.

In my early grief, a book like this might've collected dust. Throughout those days, the loss was too heavy and painful to consider picking up or understanding anything new. But eventually, the day arrived when I became ready.

I trust that you will know when you're ready to find the meaning of your grief with the help of this book.

For the next 6-weeks of pages, you'll find creative ideas for taking things one day at a time, each day providing a recipe to explore finding comfort throughout your grieving process.

Most of all, I pray that you'll be able to feel God's presence in the middle of your circumstances, whatever those circumstances may be.

If all you take from this book is one reminder, I hope it is this: your coat of grief really does become lighter and lighter as each day passes.

INTRODUCTION

PS - For Those Comforting Someone in Grief

If this is you, thank you.

Far too many people are ill-prepared or uncomfortable with another's grief, and so they stay away or do nothing.

If you're seeking how to be better equipped to provide comfort and come alongside someone actively grieving, I encourage you to go through this devotional on behalf of your loved one. By the end of 6 weeks, you'll have a greater capacity for empathizing with and understanding their journey.

Grief is a solo journey; everyone forges their way through it. However, there are universal components to the experience of the grieving process. Your loved one will likely appreciate your effort to understand and connect, even through pages in a book.

As you read through each week, please remember that often, all that's required to comfort someone in grief is simply being there. Sitting quietly, reading to them, holding them while they cry, watching movies, doing the dishes, or decorating their empty Christmas tree–are acts of quiet love that can feel so big. I know this because those simple things were done for me when I was freshly shocked in grief. I'll never forget.

Thank you again.

Let's Get Started

WEEK ONE: FINDING MEANING IN EMPTY PLACES

"When you [lose someone], it feels like the hole in your gum when a tooth falls out. You can chew, you can eat, you have plenty of other teeth, but your tongue keeps going back to that empty place, where all nerves are still a little raw."

Jodi Picoult

ONE
ROOTS BY THE STREAM

"If a flower can flourish in the desert, you can flourish anywhere."

Matshona Dhliwayo

For me, the desert climate has always been a place to avoid. First, I hate hot weather, and no amount of describing this landscape as "it's dry heat" changes my mind.

It's just too hot. God bless the many who thrive in oppressive heat as they find ways to adapt, like staying indoors.

I share that to say I've lived with a desert for years in my heart. Grief has a way of drying up the atmosphere inside a person, turning the lush and lovely pieces of life into dry and blowing sand. The heat of loss can shrivel and sear once thriving places of life and relationships. It often feels like a new thing will never grow in the drought days of loss.

In a season of thirsty, sweltering loss, the only way to survive is to get through it. There's no formula to follow except keep going. That advice is often easier to give than to follow. The geography of the desert climate has arid and sparse vegetation due to such little rainfall each year and extreme temperatures.

It's a hostile place, yet my grief plopped me right in the middle of a dune of loss. I didn't want to be there or even visit, but the death of a son, then the death of a husband, and then cancer gave me a ticket to my inner desert. I felt empty, crushed, and sad, confused as to why my life took so many exit ramps off the road I had planned.

Grief can be a place where the rubber meets the road. To survive and eventually thrive when loss hits you, look for the hidden diamond gems of help that are concealed in unexpected places. You may not see the gems at first, but they are there as flecks of glitter in your sandy spots. The morning my little boy died, a sister-in-law showed up with cleaning supplies in hand. She informed me many people would come to the house, and she tasked herself to make my bathrooms sparkle.

God knows the season you find yourself, no matter how dry and dusty it feels. Days watered by tears and a heavy heart can be soothed by knowing God will collect these times and use them to strengthen you. He is the master re-builder. God can reshape and remake your fractured or shattered pieces, no matter how broken or dry your circumstances. He cares for you in your land of drought.

Sometimes, a dry, quiet place is just the spot God wants us to be. It's a place where we can hear His soft, gentle voice. The desert demands a focus on survival. One must be prepared if they spend a lot of time there. The sun overhead can be brutal, and water and food are scarce. The desert requires provision.

Why would God allow our souls to be forced into dry, uninhabitable places when life has taken our breath away? I learned the answer to that colossal question; there often is no answer.

We live in a fallen world where sin and wrong and hard things happen. God sees but doesn't cause. He will, however, use these times when our heart is plowed up with pain to teach us about Himself.

FINDING THE MEANING OF GRIEF

No matter how broken life is, God will use the combination of where you are now and where these days will take you to melt them into lessons learned no other way. If you are in a drought now, let the Lord refresh and pour the cool drink of peace.

"But blessed is the man who trusts in the Lord, whose confidence is in Him. He will be like a tree planted by the water that sends out its roots by the stream. It does not fear when heat comes; its leaves are always green. It has no worries in the year of drought and never fails to bear fruit."

Jeremiah 17:7-8 NIV

A stream is a constant flow of water. The verse above doesn't say the tree is planted by a puddle but a stream that brings fresh supply daily. If we plant ourselves in the water of God, His provision will water us when the heat of hard times hits us.

TRY THIS: JOURNAL GOD'S CARING FOR YOU

No matter how scorched and dry you feel, lean back to rest in God's shade of provision. He has scattered precious gems of help all around you. Notice them. He is the living water that can satisfy and fill the thirst made in days of grief.

The verse below is a promise of provision. Try journaling or writing about how this provision applies to you to act on this promise. Here are a few prompts to get you started:

- Are you in a season of wilderness or drought?
- How has God cared for you in the past, or is caring for you now?
- What type of gems has He scattered all around you?
- If journaling is not an option today, maybe you can find a moment to share and discuss these questions with someone close to you.

"I cared for you in the wilderness, in the land of burning heat."

Hosea 13:5 NIV

TWO
CONNECTING WITH SOLITUDE

"Each tree grows alone, murmurs alone, thinks alone."

Willa Cather

"Solitude is pleasant. Loneliness is not."

Anna Neagle

BEING ALONE vastly differs from being lonely, yet confusing the two concepts is easy. Aloneness is solitude; loneliness is a feeling of isolation from others.

I've been "alone" for almost 15 years since my husband died. As a single person again, it took some reframing and letting go to learn how to maneuver the new life as a widow. I didn't simply become the person I was before marriage. I had stepped out of that function to become a wife, a mother, a married person. The aspects of those pieces of me developed as I blossomed to take on the roles and duties.

I had a hard time figuring out who I was without my husband. I had to fill up my days and long evenings. Not only that but eventually, I got brave enough to eat dinner out as a party of one. I had to do all the driving and take out the trash. I had to fix things I didn't know how to fix and hang the picture frames on walls.

I was alone, yes. But was I lonely? Sometimes. Still today, I notice couples—driving together, sitting in church, taking walks, sharing a meal, and doing errands together. At times, I do miss the natural companionship.

My grief prompted learning to share those times with new friends in the same solo boat. My world has expanded to know and depend on more people. I have close friends now that I would not necessarily have had were it not for the grief I've endured.

Grief showed me that we all need someone, and we all need each other.

Being lonely is an emotional state of feeling disconnected from other people. It's a natural mood but can become a dark hole you don't want to fall into. A lonely feeling can overwhelm and make a hard situation even harder. The sadness of loneliness can be felt even when surrounded by other people. That's where being alone and being lonely, part ways.

If you are having an alone day today, make the most of it. Sleep in or stay up late. Eat popcorn in bed while reading a great book, or take a glass of wine in a bubble bath. I've learned to enjoy the solitude of being alone and filling time with things I appreciate.

God is in our alone hours, for sure. He cherishes these times with you. He longs to hear your concerns and desires. Not only that, but he bends an ear close when we cry out in desperation or anger. God wants to know you trust Him enough to share hurts and joys.

God doesn't want us just to make requests. He is not a "Santa in the sky." Instead, He longs to hear us share our authentic selves. In doing so, we can establish a friendship with the One who will never leave and loves us more than we know.

Connect with God when you're feeling lonely, not just alone. He already knows everything about you. The feeling of isolation that comes with loneliness doesn't need to overtake you. If you let Him restore you, God can lift you out of that pit. Ask Him.

Are you alone today (by yourself) or lonely (feeling disconnected from others)? Remember, God can know you and fill you with His presence. He longs to give purpose to your day today. There's a word in Scripture, *dismayed*; we don't hear much in conversation, but it has a weight that describes heavy hurts.

To be dismayed is described as feeling discouraged or disconcerted by fear or alarm. Being dismayed brings worry, anxiety, or frustration. God tells us in the Word that He will strengthen and hold us up when those feelings hit. Trust Him for that; it's a remedy for loneliness.

"So do not fear, for I am with you, do not be dismayed, for I am your God. I will strengthen you and help you; I will uphold you with my righteous right hand."

Isaiah 41:10 NIV

TRY THIS: LOOK TO CONNECT

Others around us might be in the same boat of loneliness or aloneness. There are countless ways to find ourselves in this boat. Whatever the reason, connection to each other can lift us all.

Today, explore the meaning of *your* grief by making new connections, no matter how small. Some ideas for sparking connection are:

- Having coffee with a friend
- Scheduling a lunch with a colleague
- Speak a kind word of encouragement to a stranger
- Bake cookies for a neighbor
- {Or add your own idea here!}

THREE
ANGER HACKS

"To heal a wound you must stop scratching it."

Paulo Coelho

"The moment you accept what troubles you've been given, the door will open."

Rumi

THERE IS purpose found in everything if you look for it. There can be meaning even in pain.

Suffering, no matter the cause, makes deep cuts in our soul that wound and hurt. Pain in life is inevitable; it can't be avoided. It sneaks in as an unwelcome visitor that can surprise us and change life as we know it, sometimes instantly. We have all known hurt. It takes a toll, whether emotional, physical, or spiritual hurt. We become wounded. It's possible to walk around in everyday life, bearing excruciating suffering. We hide behind routine, responsibilities, isolation, and even depression.

Hurt is a generic covering caused by a smorgasbord of causes. Grief is often the umbrella that our hurt lives under. Grief is a natural reaction to any loss and hurt. The pain can feel overwhelming and crushing. They say time heals all wounds, but some heart injuries change us forever. We heal because we change. It's a choice to be made. We learn to live with the hole our loss makes and leaves inside our world. It becomes a constant reminder that we know love or, in some cases, know rejection or abandonment.

When hurt fills your heart, you can become angry and bitter or accept the circumstance, no matter how painful, and look to how it can strengthen you. These may seem like empty cliché choices, but truth be told, when grief and hurt are boiled down to a place of syrupy reduction, acceptance is the only way to grow around hurt.

Being angry, especially anger pointed towards God, is a normal reaction. Often, He's the only one or the best one to blame for loss and unfair hurt. He knows all about it.

Angry at God, A Poem by Jessica Shaver, Time of Singing, 1989

I told God I was angry.
I thought He'd be surprised.
I thought I'd kept hostility
quite cleverly disguised.
I told the Lord I hated Him.
I told Him that I hurt.
I told Him that He isn't fair,
He's treated me like dirt.
I told God I was angry
But I'm the one surprised.
"What I've known all along," He said,
"You've finally realized."
At last you have admitted
what's really in your heart.
Dishonesty, not anger
was keeping us apart.
"Even when you hate Me
I don't stop loving you.
Before you can receive that love
You must confess what's true.
"In telling Me the anger
You genuinely feel,
it loses power over you,
permitting you to heal."
I told God I was sorry
And He's forgiven me.
The truth that I was angry
has finally set me free.

TRY THIS: ANGER HACKS

Anger can stay inside you, no matter how justified or long it's rooted in your heart. Processing this very internal feeling sometimes helps to externalize it physically.

1. Identify and describe a big piece of your hurt visually with shapes and drawn images on paper. Words are optional. Sometimes, the hurt can't be described with anything but a mess of scribbles and jumble of colors.
2. Use scissors to cut the paper into as many pieces as possible. You can do this haphazardly or deliberately, whichever you feel honors your anger most appropriately.
3. Then, place the pieces into an envelope addressed to God.
4. Keep it displayed as a reminder that you can control your anger. (On the bathroom counter, in the center console of your car, next to the coffee maker, in your purse or laptop bag)

I've had days filled with emotions that only God could understand. Give him the pieces of hurt or anger you looked at today. Have faith that He knows, sees, and understands your pain.

"He heals the brokenhearted and binds up all their wounds."

Psalm 147:3 NIV

FOUR
DANCING WITH DISAPPOINTMENT

"The beauty is that through disappointment you can gain clarity, and with clarity comes conviction and true originality."

Conan O'Brien

DISAPPOINTMENT IS impossible to avoid during life. It lurks out there in the promise of what we hope for or want. As we all know, often, things don't turn out as we wish they would. We have a preconceived notion of a circumstance, and reality doesn't match up. Disappointment is that deflated feeling when other people don't measure up or let us down. We can even disappoint ourselves when we set a goal and fall short.

Make no mistake; disappointment will find you and try to sink you like a capsized boat. Things feel turned upside down, out of order, and heavy. Disappointment lives in a dry and empty place. It can lead you in your mood to feel sorry for yourself or downright frustrated.

Even the slightest disappointment can catch us off guard and set us back, no matter the size of the unmet expectation. Scripture paints a similar picture for us in the Song of Solomon. Even the smallest foxes can wreak havoc in a vineyard.

"Catch us the foxes, the little foxes that spoil the vines, for our vines have tender grapes."

Song of Solomon 2:15 NKJV

Although a few tasty grapes chewed up by a couple of crafty foxes aren't noticeable, when a pack of hungry foxes attacks the tender shoots of a spring vineyard harvest, there's a serious problem. Those of us who've experienced grief are vulnerable to the small issues of disappointment that can seem harmless. When added up, these little foxes and issues with disappointment can leave us bitter and regretful, ultimately doing harm, even unintentional harm.

Hard as it is for me to admit, on some days, the most significant lessons are learned from defeat or disappointment.

Once a disappointment has happened, it's so easy to look back and imagine all the "what ifs," wondering how a situation would have or should have turned out. While there's nothing inherently wrong with asking "what if?" it is possible to be unknowingly victimized by or stuck in our disappointment. There's no way of going back in time. (This is also a hard admission on some days.)

On the other hand, it is also possible to dance with our disappointment. In this way, our grief gets enough space to transform into new things. Dancing with disappointment doesn't make the hurt any less painful but teaches us how to hear the music differently.

TRY THIS: DANCE WITH DISAPPOINTMENT

In today's journal prompts, consider what your life might look like if you chose to "dance with" disappointment, no matter how long ago or the size of the disappointment.

- How might a new perspective of understanding change your focus on this disappointment?
- What prohibits you from hearing the whispers of truth or creativity that the Heavenly Father inspires?
- If your disappointment could talk, what would it say?
- If you could speak to your disappointment, what would you say?
- How has "what if" shown up lately?

When you finish your journal prompt(s), ask the Lord to reveal new ways to "dance with" this particular disappointment. Ask Him what He wants you to do with it. Jot down whatever insight may arise throughout your day.

> *"Trust in the LORD with all your heart and lean not on your own understanding; in all your ways acknowledge Him, and He will make your path straight."*
>
> Proverbs 3:5-6 NIV

> *"And we know that in all things God works for the good of those who love Him, who have been called according to His purpose."*
>
> Romans 8:28 NIV

FIVE
PUNCHING DOWN ON PAIN

"Although the world is full of suffering, it is full also of the overcoming of it."

Helen Keller

WHEN WE GET HURT, it's natural to feel pain. Pain is in the flavor profile of any grief. Emotional pain can be just as physical and debilitating as the physical pain that bores deep. It's intense, fierce, and grabs you by the heart with claws that cut and tear your insides.

As my late husband suffered from cancer, I had no frame of reference for his kind of debilitating pain. Sleep became too uncomfortable when the cancer reached his bones. He shared how the hours crept so slowly as he waited for morning.

I did my best to empathize, but it was hard to relate truly. Even after surviving my own battle with cancer years later, I can still only imagine how his cancer must've felt. His pain was not mine. Our physical pain was hardly comparable. I survived my cancer. He did not.

Similarly, it's hard to relate to someone's grief if it isn't yours. Like physical pain, grief is a trial no one can understand unless experienced firsthand.

Pain, from whatever source, has a way of hiding and can explode out of the boundaries of your heart. This is true for a broken bone or a broken heart. Left untended, pain can make life bitter. Pain can grow bigger into a mound of suffering without stretching and reshaping it into daily life.

I see reminders of this in the kitchen. The simple bread-making ingredients require yeast, flour, water, and sugar. A bit of yeast comes alive with foam and fermentation when sprinkled into a bowl of warm water. Mix in a few cups of flour and some sugar, then place in a warm, dark spot in the kitchen. Allow enough time to pass, and the dough will explode out of the bowl.

Breadmakers say this mound is ready to be punched down with a fist. Depending on the recipe, the dough is kneaded with the palm into desired shapes for bread or rolls.

The act of pressing down and then reshaping dough in this way expels air bubbles and stretches gluten before baking in the oven. With this step, the temperature and moisture inside the dough would be smooth, creating a beautiful texture of bread. If the dough is not punched down, the bread might not rise.

Breadmakers have the wisdom to share with those who grieve; good can come if we are willing to reshape and work with pain. Otherwise, the texture of life can turn into a dense, hard, cracked, bitter, and tough experience.

Life after grief cannot rise again if we don't roll up our sleeves and punch down the dough. In bread making, this is what reactivates the ingredients and boosts flavor. The idea of reactivating our pain might sound unpleasant, but it also changes the overall experience of our grief. It prompts our grief to develop new layers of meaning.

For example, the first anniversary of my son's death was just plain sad. The thought of losing Mark was too heavy to memorialize every year in the same way, with sadness. The first recollection of this day stung, but many years later, it changed significantly. Our family decided to rename this anniversary. That day in November is now "Mark's Heaven Birthday."

We made a singular choice to punch down on the pain and reframe our loss. It stopped much of pain's fermentation, removed the annual fear of anticipation, and relieved some of the pressure of sadness. The focus changed from death to new life.

We created a new tradition of doing something together that Mark would have enjoyed. It is an intentional acknowledgment that our shared experience of grief is more than shared loss. The new tradition is now a reason to get together, remember, and make new memories in Mark's honor.

We look forward to it every year, creating a new dimension as a family.

Scripture even has a Parable about the power of yeast:

"The kingdom of heaven is like yeast that a woman took and mixed into a large amount of flour until it worked all through the dough."

Matthew 13:33 NIV

He will do that for you, too. His soft hand of forgiveness, love, and peace can take the mess of painful dough you're filled with and take the sticky out of it. He can be your overcomer, especially in those empty places.

"The Lord is near to the brokenhearted and saves the crushed in spirit."

Psalm 34:18 NIV

TRY THIS: PUNCHING DOWN

Healing is a journey that takes time and room to breathe—no matter the reason—and often, we have many layers and facets that all need to be reshaped during the healing process. We can practice finding comfort in empty places. We can also practice thinking about pain from grief and confusing times as if it were expanding, like bread dough.

You may not be ready to reframe grief in the ways my daughter and I did. You also may not want to bake a loaf of bread from scratch. While baking *can* be a therapeutic hobby, it can still be a lot of effort and time on those hard days of grief.

What might a small version of "punching down" look like for you? Try it today.

Here's an example: feel free to "steal" it. If you've been drinking out of the same glasses or mugs, an easy place to start might be replacing one or two glasses in your cupboard. Replacing them might look like getting new literal replacements, shifting the older glasses to the front so they get used more often, or trading glasses with a friend.

I always love drinking from a pretty glass. My favorite everyday glasses at home are chunky cut glass stems from the dollar store. They make for a lovely table set; many are rugged enough for a bubble bath. Garage sales and second-hand stores are filled with inexpensive choices. They make the beverage taste and look much better, too!

If that idea doesn't feel like a fit, what is one small thing you can practice reshaping today?

(Psst! The above-bolded questions make great journal prompts, too!)

SIX
LOSS BEFORE THE LOSS

"Anticipatory grief is one way people react to the knowledge that a life-changing loss will happen in the near future. Although not everyone will experience anticipatory grief, for those who do, it's a normal response to the sadness and uncertainty that impending loss brings to both the present and the future."

Scott Berinato[*]

THE READING TODAY takes a slight turn. While we have looked at many aspects of grief and how it affects us, this book's main thrust is for those who have walked through grief or those who are now moving through grief's passageways.

However, there's a side of grief that is easy to overlook: *anticipatory*

---

[*] *That Discomfort You're Feeling Is Grief. Harvard Business Review.* 2020. https://hbr.org/2020/03/that-discomfort-youre-feeling-is-grief

grief*. In other words, it is the process of grieving something that hasn't happened yet.

When a life-changing loss is ahead, the anticipated sadness can often cause a conventional grief reaction. This can be felt by the person who is expecting the impending loss of their own life, their job, marriage, their home, or any of a number of life changes. Anticipatory grief can also be experienced by the loved ones of the individual facing a life-altering circumstance. Those who watch from their own life the difficulty of stepping into the world of someone they care about can experience a mourning or grief reaction. These symptoms can look like sadness, denial, irritability, depression, avoidance, feeling stressed, indecision, or anger. All these components can be found inside grief.

Grief can rear its head any time along the journey of anticipating a loss. It becomes a way to prepare for the expected loss we see up ahead and know is coming.

For me, anticipatory grief was a trek to watch my mom melt into a person we could hardly recognize from dementia that took hold and wouldn't let go. The disease was slow-moving as it voyaged around her life and finally reduced her to a spark of her former self. We who loved her watched the loss of our mom before our very eyes. We knew decline was the road she traveled, and there was no way to stop it.

So, looking back, I mourned my mom long before she passed.

My husband's cancer was a similar trek, a different mountain. His cancer transformed him from a true Renaissance man who loved life and learning and his family more than anything into such a tiny morsel of his former self. We who lived around him knew the outcome long before it would happen, and he knew it, too.

Grieving my husband started years before he died.

Anticipatory grief, in my husband's case, felt like receiving a box in the mail, knowing its contents, and spending years to find a spot where it

---

* https://www.verywellmind.com/what-is-anticipatory-grief-5207928#citation-1

could reside alongside everything else in our house. When the moment finally showed up, I let him go. There was no more fight left, and I loved him too much for him to endure any more of his physical suffering.

Anticipatory grief can be a subtle way of preparing for the inevitable. But if you don't experience grief before the loss, that's fine too. Grief is grief, no matter its timing.

Waiting for a loss doesn't make the trial of grief any more or less painful. The season of anticipating a loss can be used to make the most of our time before the loss happens. Some of those memories can become a great treasure for understanding the meaning of anticipatory grief.

Whatever the timing of our grief, God doesn't want us to live too far in the future because He sustains us every day. He *will* strengthen us for what's up ahead, good or bad. We're made ready either way by living today and giving Him a chance to show us how our future is in His hands, no matter what.

TRY THIS: LISTING YOUR EXPECTATIONS

Today, let's list things you're anticipating in life. They could be positive or negative anticipations related to grief or not.

Sometimes, these anticipations are translated as hopes and dreams or wishes and prayers. Basically, things that have not yet happened that you expect to happen sometime in the future.

Finish the following sentences and repeat until you feel your list is complete.

> *TODAY, I'M ANTICIPATING...*
> *TODAY, I EXPECT...*

SEVEN
NEW PARKING SPOTS (RECIPE: MOM'S SWEET TEA)

"I weren't never lost, but I was bewildered a time or two."

Daniel Boone

ONCE GRIEF gains entrance into your world, life is never the same. It can slash with random precision and cut deeply, often with no way to put the pieces back together again the way they were. Grief pushes us into places we don't choose and rearranges the furniture of life until sometimes it's unrecognizable. It forces us out of a familiar space and dares to accept it.

Loss creates a wound in all of us. Each wound of loss intersects with the source of grief. Sometimes, this intersection of everyone's pain swirls into a collectively heavy grief wound. Others have their own grief issues and can produce a salt that pours into our wounds. When this happens, grief is more bitter than the initial loss. It's messy; it hurts and can leave our souls feeling dry and parched.

A cool cup of comfort can make a significant impact when grief has shriveled up your joy or peace. Living through the dry seasons of sorrow or suffering isn't easy, especially going it alone. Your grief is yours; no one can carry it for you, but it can become lighter when you are refreshed by knowing God has been there with you all along.

"O God, you are my God, earnestly I seek you; my soul thirsts for you, my body longs for you, in a dry and weary land where there is no water."

Psalm 63:1 NIV

New Parking Spots

After my husband died, I was surprised to find that choosing a parking spot at the hospital would require so much emotional elbow grease. For years, I parked in the same lot reserved for doctors. I parked there while George practiced medicine. I parked there while he was a cancer patient. I parked there as he died in hospice. But there came a day when I was no longer a doctor's wife. My connection to park in the doctor's lot was gone. I felt a very sharp pang from reality the day this fact hit.

One day, I returned to the hospital. Suddenly, it hit me that I was just another patient visiting the hospital for a doctor's appointment. I chose to punch down on my pain that day and accepted the reality of the ripple effect of loss.

My car found its new home in the visitor's lot from then on. Initially, this realization made the loss of my husband feel larger and reactivated my pain. After my appointment, I recognized the worst of that pain had subsided.

Years later, I drove myself to oncology appointments at that same hospital. My own battle with cancer would've been too heavy to hold alongside memories of my husband's lost battle with his cancer. On those days, a new parking lot provided relief, and I even felt *gratitude* for it!

Each return to the visitor's parking garage reminded me that I was fighting a new battle and was strong enough to face it. Much of that strength came from knowing I wasn't alone in the struggle; I was allowing myself to be refined and learning to trust God in my adversity. For me, that has made all the difference.

> "Unlike water or wine, even Coca-Cola, sweet tea means something. It is a tell, a tradition. Sweet tea isn't a drink, really. It's culture in a glass."
>
> Allison Glock

TRY THIS: MOM'S SWEET TEA

Here's an easy family iced tea recipe to make when you need a cool drink on a dry day. Or the bitter taste of loss requires a bit of sweetness.

My mom was from the South, and her sweet tea was legendary in our New York neighborhood. Back then, New York didn't serve sweet tea like they did in the South. If you ordered tea at a restaurant in the South, you had to specify "unsweetened," lest the wait staff deliver a bucketful of liquid sweet enough for the spoon to stand straight up.

My dad was a coach at a small college, and his players couldn't get enough of mom's tea, southern style. Among other things, her claim to fame was making this sweet tea every day.

She always made the tea in the same plastic Tupperware pitcher, which, over the years, acquired a sharp brown stained interior. The tea that wasn't finished each day went into ice cube trays, frozen as tea ice cubes. Add a melting sweet tea ice cube to a tall glass of lemony, already sweet tea, and it becomes slushy heaven. It's a real treat for all the Northerners who never had tea like that before!

In honor of my mom and to soothe those dry places you might have, or for just the day you're a little thirsty, iced tea is the ticket.

Mom's Sweet Tea

Ingredients:

- 3 or 4 tea bags
- Boiled water (8 cups makes a quart)
- Granulated Sugar ⅔ cup or to taste; stevia or honey make great alternatives to granulated sugar.
- Fresh lemon juice or fresh lemons, to taste

Directions:

1. Boil the water in a kettle or a pot on the stove. Once a rolling boil, turn off the water and let the bubbles subside.
2. Add tea bags and steep for 5-10 minutes or so. Iced tea can steep longer than hot tea since ice cubes dilute its strength. So keep that in mind when timing the strength.
3. Remove tea bags. Allow them to drip into the pot, but don't squeeze the bags, which can add bitterness.
4. Add sweetener to the hot tea and stir to dissolve. Taste at this point to get the sweetness to your liking.
5. Let the tea cool and pour over ice, either water ice cubes or tea ice cubes.
6. Serve with fresh lemon juice or fresh lemons. A pretty glass is a standout here.
7. A glass of sweet, refreshing comfort. Tah Dah!

Note: Even if you don't like sweet tea or wish you could but can't have it, I highly recommend making iced tea to your liking and freezing tea in ice cubes. Worth it!

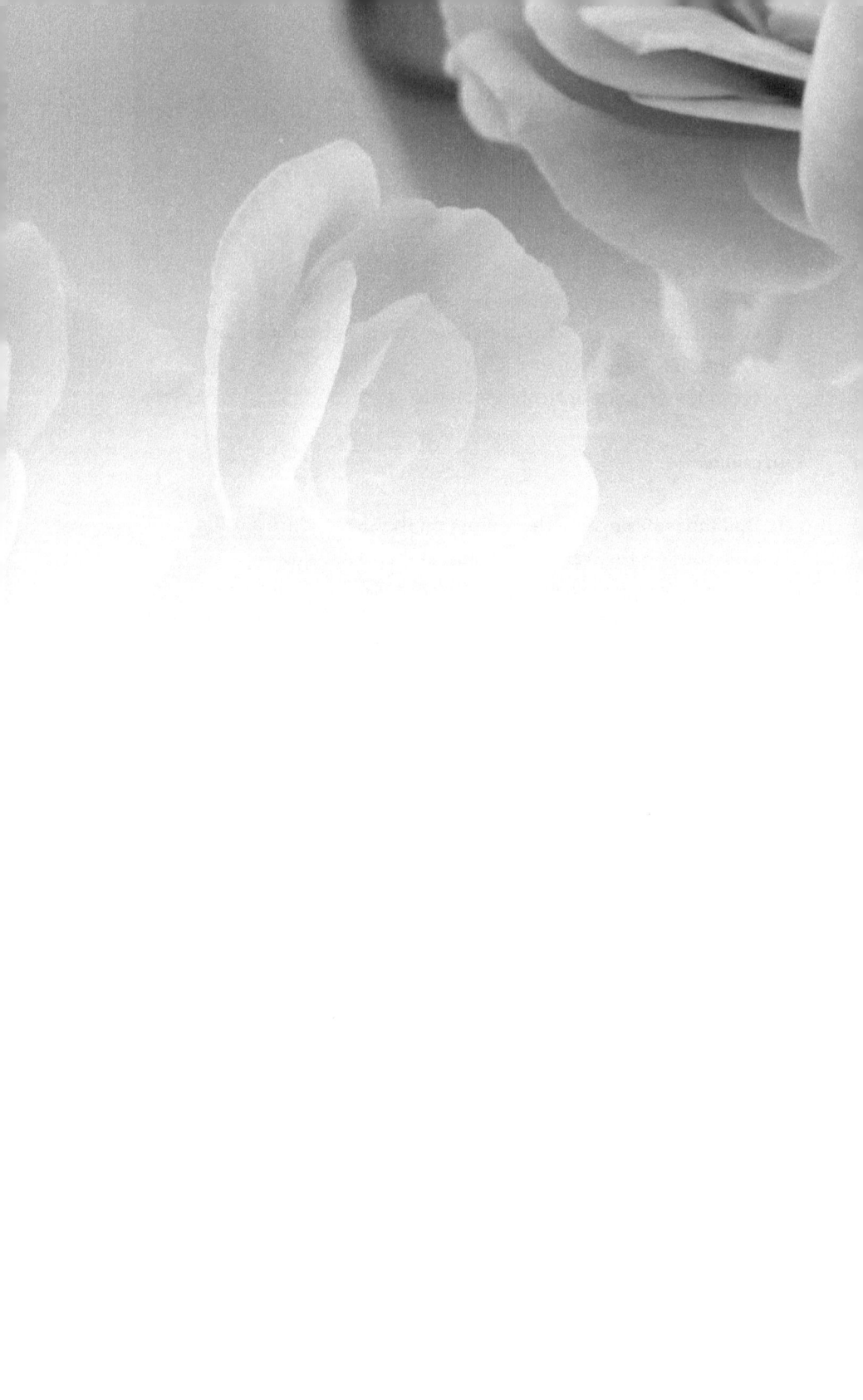

WEEK TWO: FINDING MEANING IN CHANGE

"Not everything that is faced can be changed. But nothing can be changed unless it's faced."

James Baldwin

EIGHT
REARRANGING FURNITURE & UNWANTED CHANGE

"All things must change to something new, to something strange."

Henry Wadsworth Longfellow

I HAVE a friend with a gift for home decorating. Every time I go to her house, the furniture is moved around. It cracks me up and always looks beautiful. She accepts any compliment by responding, "I needed a change."

Not everyone thrives on change. My daughter, as a kindergartener, thrived on the predictable. One day, a small amount of my rearrangement of living room furniture prompted her to dive into one of the couch cushions with exasperation. She refused to look up until I put everything back the way it was when she left for school that morning.

I remember going into her room one school night a few years later. Her clothes were meticulously laid out on the bed as if she were inside them. The shirt was tucked into the skirt on top of tights and, at the end of one long sleeve, lay a ring she planned to wear the next day. (That kind of organization and attention to detail helped her earn a doctoral degree and succeed in academia to this day!)

It's unusual to find that we *intentionally* build and strengthen skills out of our desire to avoid unwanted life changes. We are all wired uniquely and for the purpose we're created to fulfill. However, no matter our internal design or external demands, change happens to us, especially unwanted change. But not all change is like furniture that can get put back to where it used to be.

Unwanted change can hurt us. It cuts with random precision that feels personal and unique.

The definition of *unwanted* has no hidden understanding; it means something or someone is not wanted. A particular circumstance is undesirable or unwelcome. At some level, we have these occurrences from birth: a hungry baby crying or a three-year-old tantrum not wanting to share; it's easy to recognize early on that life isn't smooth or without trials. However, there comes a time when the sucker punch of grief from loss, abandonment, and unwanted change hits hard, which doubles us over. These are the days when feeling overwhelmed or fearful comes naturally.

Just because we don't want something doesn't guarantee it won't happen. Sheer willpower can't stop the unstoppable. Yet, choice is a tool to accept unwanted changes. When you utilize the power of acceptance, you can face the hard things and look change straight in the eye. This is possible because choice plows through unwanted change when we accept it.

Accepting unwanted changes isn't the same as *approving* the unwanted changes. Acceptance, not approval, is how you can choose to see the light at the end of your painful tunnel, no matter how dim it appears now.

For many of us, our unwanted circumstances will always remain unwanted. Health diagnoses, company layoffs, business failures, global recessions, relationship breakups, etc. This was the case for many of the life changes I've experienced. I would never choose them for anyone, but I can't deny that they happened, and I knew I had to accept them. I didn't have to like or approve of them. Accepting unwanted changes isn't the same as *approving* the unwanted changes.

The grieving process is a great example of this kind of acceptance. It's easy to get stuck in our grief. Steeping in confusion or heartache might allow our injuries to distract us from seeing God's desired path in life. When the inevitable distractions arise, God can use them to build our faith and dependence on Him like nothing else.

If we are lost in the woods of unwanted change, the recipe forward with more comfort is this: accept the change, but don't accept it by yourself. We were created to be in community, with other people, and especially with our Heavenly Father, who cares for us more than we can imagine.

If you feel alone today, God sees your hurt. He's ready to talk about it even if you don't want to. He can give you a strategy and a plan to direct your path forward. Just ask Him.

TRY THIS: VERSE OF THE DAY

Selecting a scripture verse that speaks to you or gives encouragement or comfort is a practice that brings comfort on hard days. The verse can become a thought or statement to chew on, ponder, and become part of your spiritual tool belt to pull out when a hard time hits.

1. Today, choose a scripture about ***unwanted change***. I've provided a few of my favorites at the end of today's reading, but you are welcome to use another if you'd prefer.
2. Take a few minutes today to meditate on the word God wants you to hear today. You may approach this in whatever way you'd like.
3. Copy the verse in your journal or on a notecard to keep with you throughout the day.

4. Add today's date alongside the verse to return to it later. Noting today's date will remind you how faithful God was all along. I've always been grateful for these reminders of His provision.
5. Consider your chosen verse and answer the questions below or in your journal.

THE VERSE I CHOSE TODAY IS...
I CHOSE THIS VERSE BECAUSE...

- What is God asking you to change, understand, or be comforted by?
- Why does this particular verse add meaning to your grief?
- How will you receive or accept this new meaning?

"Be Joyful always; pray continually; give thanks in all circumstances, for this is God's will for you in Christ Jesus."

1 Thessalonians 5:16 NIV

"Do not be anxious about anything, but in everything, by prayer and petition, with thanksgiving, present your requests to God. And the peace of God, which transcends all understanding, will guard your hearts and your minds in Christ Jesus."

Philippians 4:6-7 NIV

"I have told you these things, so that in me, you will have peace. In this world, you will have trouble. But take heart! I have overcome the world."

John 16:3 NIV

_____

_____

"So do not fear, for I am with you; do not be dismayed, for I am your God. I will strengthen you and help you; I will uphold you with my righteous right hand."

Isaiah 41:10 NIV

_____

NINE
DEEP WATERS OF PREPARATION

"A bend in the road is not the end of the road... Unless you fail to make the turn."

Helen Keller

I'VE NOTICED my tendency to be more prepared with every year that passes. I now try on clothes before packing for a trip to determine if I want to bring them and if they still fit. You'll find my pantry stuffed with food and essentials just in case the power goes out. The 12 pounds of coffee stashed in the basement's food shelf might never get used. Still, it is ready, along with two solar power generators, multiple packs of batteries, and twenty-eight dinner plates in case any company shows up.

For many of us who've experienced grief or the trauma of sudden loss, **we have a desire and need to be prepared for the unexpected,** consciously or not, trying to anticipate what's required to avoid difficulties ahead. It's an act of self-preservation for those moments when we aren't warned of a change that might smack across our lives. We don't want to look up and see a door we've never walked through without having metaphorical flashlights ready.

In many circumstances, **there would be no way to prepare.** It would require more than anyone could fathom. Those changes bite suddenly and deeply, ultimately deforming and distorting our lives and world. No one could be prepared for that. In those moments, we would all be ill-prepared and ill-equipped.

No class, no workshop, no degree, no basement food shelf, and no parenting expert could've prepared me for the horror of waking up one morning to find that my 9-year-old son had died in his sleep. Anyone would be unprepared and ill-equipped for something like that.

Perhaps you have a similar moment of feeling ill-equipped in your life. These are the moments that leave their marks on us. Any loss, especially the devastating ones, strands us in uncharted waters. Navigation can seem impossible.

When my family rolled out of bed that morning, it was unimaginable that we'd spend the afternoon driving around town shopping for burial plots. Much of that day still feels like a blur, each flash enormous and overwhelming.

These are the deep waters that require complete surrender. But not the surrender of giving up; the surrender is to realize some circumstances are completely out of our control. By surrendering, we relinquish our need to understand the "why" of a particular suffering.

God sees the situations that have broken us and promises to walk beside each of us through the pain. Physical, emotional, or spiritual pain is suffering that confronts us all in due time; it's a human experience.

We can't see what's ahead, but we can trust the one who can. While God doesn't cause suffering, He sees it and can help us travel through it. Hurt is certainly out there, and my name is on more to come, but I know I won't be stepping into it alone.

"He heals the brokenhearted and binds up their wounds."

John 147:3 NIV

Anticipated or not, a question will arise after any kind of loss or hurt. "What's next?" It hit hard every time, at least it did for me, and it certainly hit our family hard on that day. Amidst the fog of funeral plans, I heard myself and others say, "What do we do *next?*"

Questions like these are particularly crushing when we could never fully prepare for the enormity of the event in the first place.

Unlike the sudden loss of my son, our family's experience with my husband's long battle with cancer was different. I look back on that time as both a fight and a loss we eventually anticipated. Once we had set our minds and hearts on his impending passing, in reality, we would never have been ready to say goodbye.

Accepting the reality of their deaths is not the same as understanding the reason for their deaths, if any. Eventually, I reached a point of relinquishing my need to know, "Why me? Why them?" I would never know why, and I reached a place where I fully accepted that.

Through this acceptance and surrender of my need to understand, I found space to explore the meaning of my grief. Grief is not death. Grieving is not equivalent to dying, although it may feel like it on some days. Reaching this acceptance bolstered my faith, which I can accept without understanding fully.

"We live by faith, not by sight."

2 Corinthians 5:7 NIV

Part of the meaning of *my* grief from the loss of my husband and son was letting go of the life I once envisioned with them. Unrealized hopes and dreams drop from our hands with silent crashes.

No, we can't prepare for everything and anything. We can't see what's ahead, but our Heavenly Father, who knows us by name, is already there. I like to think of Him standing at the end of our lives, looking back to where we're walking now. If we keep our eyes on Him, He'll walk us through whatever pitfalls may lie in waiting ahead. The key is keeping our focus on Him.

Hurt is certainly out there, and I know my name is on more grief to come, but I'm not afraid to step up to it because God was faithful throughout the past hard times to help me get through. I trust Him to be faithful again every day.

Being unprepared for what grief brings to life can be a confusing tangle of knots that hurt to untie. We can't be prepared for everything, but we can have faith to draw closer to our Savior, which grows perseverance and acceptance.

"Consider it pure joy, my brothers and sisters, whenever you face trials of many kinds, because you know that the testing of your faith produces perseverance"

James 1:2-3 NIV

TRY THIS: A WRITING PROMPT

In the space below, consider the journal prompt. Use the question as a springboard for your thoughts to take shape. Writing without self-editing is a great way to let places in your heart and mind speak to you.

- Sit in a quiet place and get relaxed. This exercise can be as long or short as it happens. Bring to mind a change you've

experienced where you felt unprepared—small or large. If there is more than one, choose the one that appears first.
- Close your eyes and picture the change with as much detail as possible. Note any physical changes inside your body that arise, like a thumping heart or sad feeling. That's okay.
- Take a few deep breaths. Put your pen on the paper.
- Don't think about your writing as you go or make corrections. Just write. Let the words flow out, even if you write one thought for the whole page.
- Start by finishing this sentence:

I WASN'T READY FOR _____, BUT I'M WILLING TO ACCEPT _____...

TEN
COMPARING APPLES TO LASAGNA

"There are many points in life when we cannot see what awaits us around the corner, and it is precisely at such times, when our path forward is unclear, that we must bravely keep our nerve, resolutely putting one foot before the other as we march blindly into the dark."

Richard C. Morais, *The Hundred-Foot Journey*

WHEN LOSS HIT MY LIFE, I had no idea the changes that loomed up ahead with my name written on it. The words of loss and sadness were scrolled in bold and large print. I knew I had changed completely in an unknowable way. At first, I had no clue how challenging life would feel with my heart full of so much grief. We don't realize what a precious gift life is until it's gone. I regret how often I took time for granted.

My little boy loved to lay on the couch with me, snuggled under a blanket together. He called it having "covers." There were so many times I brushed the request off to do some task I deemed more important, like vacuuming or dishes. What I would give now to have just one more time of "covers." Who knew his life would be cut so short? The thing is, we never know.

We're each given a certain time on earth, some only nine years, some over 90. Scripture tells us,

---

"You have decided the length of our lives. You know how many months we will live, and we are not given a minute longer."

Job 14:5 NLT

God provides important information we need. Our days are determined. That sobering fact can change how we wake up each morning. Every morning, we open our eyes, another day is given, and we make the most of it. He has divine appointments ready and people He needs us to help, speak to, or encourage. We have a purpose much bigger than ourselves. Our days matter, even in days of grief or confusion.

"Teach us to make the most of our time so that we may grow in wisdom."

Psalm 90:12 NLT

That's the thing about grief. We don't know what to expect once it calls our name and smacks us in the heart. Often, with such force, our breath is knocked out. It's a pain that only those who have experienced it can really understand.

My grief is no harder than yours to bear.

This comparison would be like comparing apples to lasagna. The struggles I have faced are no more difficult than yours are; my griefs are just that, mine. Your griefs are yours, not mine.

Grief presents unique pain to each of us, depending on the cause. For example, when a husband remarries after the death of his first wife, he may have lost his first wife and started a new relationship with a second wife. The relationship role of "wife" is now filled for this man, but any children from his first marriage can never replace their mom.

The grief of loss is unique, depending on the relationship.

A mom loses her son when a little boy dies, but the boy's sister loses a brother. Losing the same person can feel like the loss of a different person for each of us. When a co-worker loses their job, a boss loses an employee, and the remaining co-workers lose their friends. When a patriarch dies, one generation loses their father; another generation loses their grandpa.

Understanding the variety and nuance surrounding each loss can deepen the meaning of our grief.

When my husband died, I lost a life partner and best friend; my daughter lost her Dad. We both experienced the loss of the same family member, but our individual experiences were entirely unique and based on very different relationships. I became caught up in my own circle of loss, and so did she. These two different circles of loss were expressed in our own distinctive way.

Often, we don't know how to cope with a type of pain because it is so uniquely our own.

If I were to switch places with my daughter, at the time of my husband's death, I hadn't yet lost my father, so I couldn't fully understand my daughter's grief. Similarly, she was in college and didn't know what it was like to lose a husband. Of course, her loss was as big as mine, just a different relationship.

Too often, our eyes get so stuck on our hurts and circumstances that we miss the meaning and blessing that comes from an empathetic understanding of those around us. We may not know exactly how the life changes will unfold for us now, but we can choose to notice the new circles of community and support that appear.

When change brings the unknown, it also brings the opportunity to step outside a box of familiarity. Often, once familiar, life looks entirely new. Acts of service can become your recipe for finding a new comfort zone, especially when the once familiar is suddenly unfamiliar.

Not only are acts of service a spiritual practice, but they are an intentional practice to reacquaint yourself with a new life or a new version of your life. Peter said we can use our God-given gifts to serve others,

> *"Each one should use whatever gift he has received to serve others, faithfully administering God's grace in its various forms."*
>
> 1 Peter 4:10 NIV

We are uniquely wired with our personality, temperament, and distinctive talents. God designed us for a remarkable purpose, desiring us to serve others. Even in our deepest suffering, looking outside our pain has benefits. By serving others, we are served. By loving others, we are loved, and by forgiving others, we are forgiven—such simple words with such depth.

It's up to us to choose whether to serve ourselves or others each day. In serving others, even in small ways, we serve God and are His hands and feet here on earth. It is a privilege to take up each day's assignment and be a servant.

> *"My commandment is this: love each other as I have loved you."*
>
> John 15:12 NIV

TRY THIS: SERVING OPPORTUNITY

Look around your life and find someone to serve. Starting small is the best way to begin. Those who can barely decide what to eat for dinner can begin with whatever act of service feels doable for today.

- It might be like noticing trash on the ground and picking it up.
- Another idea might be to return an extra stray abandoned shopping cart to its collection point.
- Maybe you could ask the fast food attendant how their day's going and give them an unexpected compliment.
- Open your newspaper, and there will probably be a story that features an organization that needs a pair of helping hands.
- Your church always needs volunteers for the nursery, parking, ushering, etc. You never know the people you will serve with and who could become a new friend.
- I have a friend who volunteers at the USO lounge at our airport. She attends the check-in desk, enjoys helping the active duty service folks, and gets free airport parking.
- The same friend is a civilian volunteer for the United States Coast Guard. She helps with activities along the river that goes through our city.
- There may be a music festival, an art show, or a county fair in your area that needs some helping hands.

As you open your eyes to fresh ways to serve, you'll feel more comfortable in new surroundings. There will be opportunities all around you.

Once we start looking, it's remarkable how starved our culture is for unexpected encouragement, kindness, or help. God thinks so highly of encouragement that He tells us in the Word to do this.

"Please others, if we do what helps them, we will build them up in the Lord."

Romans 15:2 NLT

ELEVEN
NURTURING JOY WITH NEWNESS

"Taking a new step, uttering a new word, is what people fear most."

Fyodor Dostoevsky, *Crime and Punishment*

MANY PEOPLE FEEL anxious about upheaval. This is completely understandable. Add grief into an anxious mix, and the situation is ripe for fear of change to bloom and grow.

For instance, being anxious about starting a new job is natural. However, adding the component of a funeral service, losing a loved one, or processing any grief would make going to work difficult. Furthermore, a new job would be especially difficult to handle.

Fear of change is universal. It shows its face in almost everyone at one time or another. Sometimes, it's difficult to distinguish between our rational and irrational fears.

Early days of grief may be filled with a feeling of wanting to escape or run. Anxiousness from loss can overwhelm and paralyze. Fear of losing control into fits of tears or panic often keeps the grieving person from going out to familiar places.

It can take courage to go back into a normal routine when nothing will ever be the same, and it takes time for a new normal to emerge when life isn't the same anymore.

I remember the days after my little boy died, still filled with the shock of his sudden and completely unexpected death. I was angry that everyone I saw was going about life as if nothing horrible had happened. They drove cars, shopped in the grocery store, and went to the bank. I was flattened and full of so much pain that normal life didn't make sense.

I was afraid to do errands. I wasn't sure when a stab of paralyzing grief would take me to my knees, so I stayed home. But I still had a household to run, a daughter and husband who were dealing with the same loss as I, each of us floating in our separate circles of paralysis. It seemed like there was no place for us to intersect except through our deep pain.

It took the urging of good friends around me and encouraging me to leave the house. We started playing tennis. The routine of hitting something, a tennis ball, gave my fear and pain a place to go. It took some time, but I slowly came around and laid down my fear of the sudden change. Our family eventually learned to live life around the hole that my son's death created.

The loss was not minimized, but our grief turned into a new strength for our family. I started to see God's hand on my heart. I had a new empathy for others in pain because I knew what it felt like. God did not waste our family's suffering. Your suffering will never be wasted when you let Him use it for good.

God's word has a lot to say about the goodness of change.

Deep in the middle of loss or heartbreak, it's challenging to consider goodness about anything, especially unwanted change that causes fear.

The goodness at the most basic level is that God's presence is always with us, even if we can't feel it or want it. I didn't want to hear that it would get better. I didn't want anyone to tell me that. During moments of grief, I couldn't imagine what a "better" life could be when I was going through the worst thing, something unimaginable. But God's love and comfort are present with us during those times.

He lessens the fear and pain by pouring His grace and hope into our broken places. He uses time to allow us to adjust to the changes that we fear. Choosing to work with him, not against him, is akin to what Scripture says,

---

"So don't worry about tomorrow, for tomorrow will bring its own worries. Today's trouble is enough for today."

Matthew 6:34 NLT

TRY THIS: NURTURING JOY WITH NEWNESS

After any loss, taking the first steps towards facing the way life is now takes courage and determination. It's easy to let ourselves get or stay stuck with feet planted, afraid to move forward.

Even a small "yes," like agreeing to hit tennis balls with my friends, took more bravery than I knew I had. But once I was on the court a few times, I realized what a joy it was to do something outside my normal routine.

Today, think of something you could try, something new that would allow a step into a fresh thing.

- Visit a dog park and enjoy the fun, even if you don't have a dog.
- Volunteering for a local foster animal organization or spending the afternoon with animals can make anyone smile.

- If you're inclined, get a friend to hit tennis balls or a bucket of golf balls with you.
- If you're a "shower person," take a bubble bath and bring a glass of something yummy.
- Curl on the couch with a new magazine under a cozy throw.
- Take your kids or grandkids on a new outing that will make everyone smile.
- Try out a new recipe and invite a friend to dinner.
- Check out a new-to-you store.

Today, I encourage you to choose a little joy while easing into your new changes.

TWELVE
REORDERING SPACE & RELATIONSHIPS

"We learn by rearranging what we know."

Ludwig Wittgenstein

EVERYONE HAS a timeline for integrating past versions of themselves into the present. My time sequence is no more correct than yours; we are all unique.

For instance, a widower might feel the need to sell his wife's car the week of her funeral. Seeing it every day sitting empty in the garage might hurt too much. To outsiders, selling her car this quickly might seem disrespectful and too quick of a decision. But from his perspective, this is his way of making a path to live without her.

On the other hand, it took me five years to remove my wedding band after my husband died. I wasn't ready to let go of that piece of who I once was. But one day, I looked down at my hand and knew in my heart it felt like the right time. I removed it and placed it in a box next to my engagement ring. There is still an indentation on my finger where that ring lived for those 26 years, a symbol that I had once belonged to someone as his wife.

It isn't easy reordering, moving things around, and adjusting from how things were to how things are now. However, rearrangement tends to shed light on new opportunities to add meaning to our grief if we let it.

Each step to restructure has a ripple effect that's easily missed. Nothing happens in solitude, even if we do it alone. For instance, becoming single again changes a friend pool. Often, it seems, married couples have activities with other couples. A single becomes an odd couple.

A health diagnosis or an accident thrusts you down corridors of experience you never chose. There will be caregivers and medical personnel that wouldn't ever cross your path were it not for the circumstance that hits your life.

A relationship betrayal can untie your ability to trust again. A betrayal can hurt deeply and change your perspective about people, leaving disillusionment and feelings of abandonment that influence everything.

My son, who died, had special needs. When he passed, in one day, I lost relationships with my favorite speech therapists, therapeutic swimming instructors, occupational therapy workers, Special Education teachers, and special needs school bus drivers—all of who I never saw again. They had become daily and weekly fixtures in our lives and ordered the schedule of our days. Suddenly, their services were not required. I remember feeling out of balance with the now empty hours I faced, appointments gone.

Each example mentioned takes a certain rearranging of thought and processing. For many of us, this reordering is a light on the path to our healing and another layer of added meaning.

Change is the common denominator of any loss. No matter how big or life-altering, accepting or reordering a change is part of the grieving process. One aspect of the meaning of *your* grief might be the change it brings.

Small things like selling cars, unpacking boxes, and taking off a small, simple ring that no longer holds a promise--these symbolic actions can spark clarity during seasons of surrender to unwanted change.

These are also perfect opportunities to let your faith take hold and grow. This is where Jesus can move in and repurpose your hurts and confusion. God can reassign and restyle circumstances into something entirely new. Our suffering and trials can be part of a new purpose and destiny. Nothing is ever wasted with our Savior. He'll use every drop of who we are, debris and all. He can change it into the divine. If we let Him, a little at a time, we can accept the reality of how life has moved things around.

Perhaps for you, this reordering will start by letting go of physical items. Maybe it starts by getting a fresh, new calendar and officially migrating from the old one to avoid daily reminders of a previously planned life not lived. Possibly, it will start by cleaning the closets or one singular drawer. Or perhaps you're ready to take off the ring.

At the end of the day, the meaning of your grief will likely require rearranging life.

Remember that you always get the choice to decide this meaning and co-author the rearrangement to make room for whatever is next in life. Ask God to show you how He wants you to move forward.

Try This: Switch Up a Familiar Routine

In yesterday's activity, we infused joy into new things. Today's activity is to practice switching up old, familiar routines and coming up with alternatives.

1. Make a list of ten routines, tasks, or daily moments you're willing to change, regardless of size or how boring.
2. Once you have a list of ten, select between 1-4 for today's activity. Save the others to try out on another day. (If you're looking for an extra challenge, choose the more difficult or out-of-your-comfort-zone things.)
3. For each of the selected routines, brainstorm three alternatives.

4. Pick one of each alternative to try out today!

The point of this exercise is not to find a permanent replacement for these routines. Instead, the goal is to practice letting your mind creatively try something new in a safe (and maybe wacky?) way.

Here are a few *examples* to get you started:

Have morning coffee in the same mug

- Drink it in a teacup
- Drink tea in the same mug
- Eat cereal out of that same mug instead of coffee

Brush your teeth standing at the sink

- Standing in the living room to look at a different view than normal.
- Brush your teeth sitting down.
- Brush your teeth in the shower, even if you're not running late.

Eat dinner sitting in front of the TV

- Eat dinner at the dining room table
- Eat dinner by candlelight, even if alone.
- Eat dinner at a drastically different time of day/night.

TEN ROUTINES TO POTENTIALLY SWITCH UP:

1. Routine:
2. Routine:
3. Routine:
4. Routine:
5. Routine:
6. Routine:
7. Routine:
8. Routine:

9. Routine:
10. Routine:

TODAY I'M SWITCHING UP:

1.

- Alternative 1:
- Alternative 2:
- Alternative 3:

2.

- Alternative 1:
- Alternative 2:
- Alternative 3:

3.

- Alternative 1:
- Alternative 2:
- Alternative 3:

4.

- Alternative 1:
- Alternative 2:
- Alternative 3:

THIRTEEN
DOWNSIZING & DONATION BOXES

"Some changes look negative on the surface, but you will soon realize that space is being created in your life for something new to emerge."

Eckhart Tolle

CHANGE HAS A PLEASANT SIDE, like getting a bathroom painted a whole new shade or finally hanging that framed print leaning against the wall for months. Exciting and hoped-for changes include a new car, a new baby, or getting engaged.

Personally, I couldn't be happy without at least a little change, and I have yet to meet anyone who disagrees with that. I think this is intentional. God gave us the impact of seasons, each with its own brilliance.

The weather changes. Our moods change. Change is inevitable. We have the choice to make the most of it.

I'm at a stage where I want to downsize, simplify, and get things in order. I've finally accepted that one person doesn't need 47 cloth napkins or six full sets of dishes.

My 15-month-old grandson is at the age where opening kitchen drawers and cupboards is irresistible. He discovered the large drawer with my cloth napkin collection and gleefully emptied its contents. He had a wild time, throwing them to the floor and laughing. The pile's size shocked and embarrassed me. I counted out a few favorites, and the rest went to the donation box.

In my younger days, I tended to hold on to everything, afraid of missing out. It meant a lot to me back then to collect cloth napkins, dishes, and crystal stemware; you get the drift. But as years passed, it's now more obvious what is necessary and what isn't. Age has more easily let me know what's worth treasuring and what is not.

Sometimes, we must pull everything out, take a look, and decide what's worth keeping or letting go. True for cloth napkins, true for life. There's always a season of letting go. We let go of items, unfilled dreams, people, and relationships. At times, it may feel hard to keep up.

This kind of change can look chaotic and confusing at first. Organizing closets is a perfect example of this. Completing a project like that will look like a disaster zone long before the closet looks immaculate and organized.

But if we stick with the task at hand and don't give up or turn back, then new understanding and new purpose can emerge from our messiness (and grief). At this point in the process, we get to embrace the sparkle that the mess creates.

"Praise be to the God and Father of our Lord Jesus Christ, the Father of compassion and the God of all comfort, who comforts us in all our troubles so that we can comfort those in any trouble with the comfort we ourselves have received from God"

2 Corinthians 1:3-4 NIV

I'm allowing God to teach me such new and profound things about Him and His ways through the change I've experienced. He promises to comfort us so we can comfort others. These things could only be understood in light of change, even unwanted life changes.

It's easy to get swept off our feet into the muddy water of fear and doubt. I encourage you to take hold of the One who doesn't change. God is our rock and promises to always be there for us if we ask Him.

Seek, today, the one who doesn't change.

"Jesus Christ is the same yesterday and today and forever."

Hebrews 13:8 NIV

TRY THIS: THINGS TO PONDER

We change. Circumstances change—life changes. But our God doesn't, and we can count on that, even if it seems too hard to grasp now.

Take some time for a walk or a drive. If that's not possible, find a comfortable, cozy spot to sit for a while. As you do this, ponder one of these three things.

- *If you're on a drive,* look around (safely). As your surroundings change, thank God for the ways you've noticed that He never changes.
- *If you're on a walk,* take deep breaths while humming a song or prayer of thanksgiving. Use your steps to lift your spirit with gratitude. This also pleases God.
- *If you're sitting, h*um a song or prayer of thanksgiving. Create an atmosphere of thankfulness. This also pleases God.

FOURTEEN
A NEW FAMILIAR (RECIPE: POTATO CHIP GRILLED CHEESE)

"Only in the darkness can you see the stars."

Martin Luther King Jr.

ALL DIFFERENT ASPECTS of change in life were covered throughout this week's chapter. It's a hard pill to swallow when we add grief or suffering to the mix of pain and suffering. Grief seems to choke out life and often takes our breath away.

After grief strikes, it can be shocking to admit that we are unready for anything. It can feel more shocking how difficult it is for life to reshape into something new. We are strengthened in faith by looking for His hand, soldering the old pieces into something different and useful for His glory.

Change or loss of any kind can be scary and can tie us up in knots.

Reordering life or even our thinking is not an easy task. It takes a willingness to let go or to lay down an older, familiar way of life. For example, I learned to cook for my childhood family of seven. So, cooking for a table of one doesn't often match with the serving sizes listed in my favorite recipes. In this way, I haven't yet reordered my cooking to align with my new life.

This kind of reordering and reorienting can occur in any part of life touched by grief. These are the moments when we need a compass and a sure foundation to take what was and make it into what it is now.

Grief, heavy and sticky, can hang around for a long time. Often, there isn't any way to escape the hurt from it. We take it everywhere we go. We might not notice it, but it's there waiting all the same.

Accepting change doesn't necessarily imply agreeing with a change or being particularly happy about it. Losing a job might be devastating, but that could allow a more satisfying job to appear. A health crisis, while a crisis, might be just the catalyst to changing a diet or making for a more healthy lifestyle. Not all acceptance of change has a positive result; accepting the devastating loss of a loved one or being betrayed, resulting in a messy divorce, brings changes that are not so easily accepted. Eventually, the way forward is to make the best of the way life turns out.

We don't need to do it alone. We have God's promise never to leave or forsake us, and that's a solid rock to stand on.

Don't be afraid of a "new way" now that you have experienced a circumstance that led you to read this book. There's comfort in the confusing land of change, even if it's difficult to see. God wants to know you in a more personal, more profound way. What better time than now?

For those of us who've gone through any amount of sorrow, it's a familiar feeling. Grief is going to make us sad; we know this is true. So, instead of choosing sadness as a place to park, acknowledge sadness can come with you as you go about your day.

Don't be afraid of sadness. Feelings come and go.

TRY THIS: A RECIPE — POTATO CHIP GRILLED CHEESE

Sadness is a sensation that many people are uncomfortable feeling, kind of like potato chips in a grilled cheese sandwich.

This is why I'm sharing an easy recipe for you to try today. It requires very little culinary skill and, I hope, will bring a smile to your tummy. I like combining ingredients that don't seem to go together but pair quite nicely.

The hidden treasure of this new-to-you recipe is the familiar crunch from your favorite potato chips. If you make these, I encourage you to treat this like another opportunity to practice doing familiar things in new ways.

Grilled cheese sandwiches are a staple in my house. There's something comforting about melted cheese between any kind of bread. I've made an open-face grilled cheese for breakfast, a ham and pickle filled grilled cheese for lunch, and have even tried grilled cheese with fresh spinach filling for a dinner selection. No matter how elevated, there's no wrong time to eat food you remember from childhood.

When thinking of a change in your life now, this will often bring discomfort. Many of us balance these feelings by seeking out comfort in countless forms. One of my go-to places of comfort is the kitchen for an easy-to-eat sandwich. The recipe below is especially comforting when I'm feeling a little blue and need to remind myself that switching things up is okay.

When grief hits, we're often forced to do an *old* thing in a *new* way. Everything can feel like it must be reformulated in a *new* way. The unfamiliar will eventually make its trek into a place that feels normal, no matter how long the hallway to get there seems. Don't be reluctant to try something new; it might be just the right fit for the place you find yourself in now.

Filling the inside of a grilled cheese sandwich with potato chips might seem a wacky combination, but give it a try. You can always redo the sandwich, skip the interior crunch, and fill your plate with crispy chips. Either way, the duo works.

"Reading one book is like eating one potato chip."

Diane Duane

Potato Chip Grilled Cheese

Makes 1 Sandwich

Ingredients:

- Cheese
- Sliced cheese of choice: Cheddar, American, Colby, or a combo of any kind
- Sliced bread: Ciabatta, Wheat, Sturdy White, Rye—whatever is a favorite
- Potato Chips: Kettle, Groovy, or BBQ. Your favorite flavor. Firm chips work best.

How To:

1. Melt enough butter over medium heat until bubbly, to the diameter of your bread slices. Watch that it doesn't burn.
2. Add two slices of bread to the butter. Move the bread across the melted butter pool to coat each slice's bottom. Place cheese slices on each piece of bread and watch for the cheese to get soft and melt. (The sandwich starts with an open face, then the cheese melts.)
3. Top one slice of bread with potato chips, fitting them as you like.
4. When the cheese is soft and melty on each slice, turn off the heat and place the not potato chip slice of the sandwich on top of the chip-loaded side. Give a light press and remove from the pan to a cutting board or plate.

5. Cut in half and see the gooey melted cheese and crunchy potato chip center.

ENJOY!

WEEK THREE: FINDING MEANING IN YOUR JOURNEY

"The rain will stop, the night will end, the hurt will fade. Hope is never so lost that it can't be found."

Ernest Hemmingway

FIFTEEN
SINKING SAND

"Set my feet on a rock and give me a firm place to stand."

Psalm 40:2 NIV

WHEN A SEASON OF GRIEF HITS, no matter the cause, it can feel like sinking into the sand. Don't be fooled if you should ever encounter quicksand on an outdoor adventure. It appears as if it can hold the weight of a person walking across it, but take only a few steps into its quagmire, and you'll find yourself in a frightening situation.

Quicksand, when encountered, looks solid when undisturbed but behaves partially like a gel. However, even when a small pressure is applied to its particles, the loose sand and soil, oversaturated by water, will liquefy and quickly cause an object to sink or get trapped.

Grief is similarly deceiving. An acquaintance or observer of your life might assume that all is well, steady, and okay. As one grieves, it's easy to mask everything hidden under the surface. But the reality of daily grief can feel like standing in quicksand, trapped by crushing pressure. The harder the struggle, the heavier it feels, the tighter its grasp.

For some, flailing in grief can pull down to unsteady and shaky places where nothing seems solid or secure. For others, this grief might overtake them, inspiring doubts about survival. These are precarious and uniquely personal times, with an entanglement of confusion and sadness inside. Please take it seriously and ask for help if you're in that place.

If trapped in quicksand, the only way to be rescued is to move your legs very slowly and turn onto your back to float flat on top of it. Put into spiritual terms, if you're flailing and calling for help, you might not be able to hear those who answer. God wants us to do that as well with grief. The way out is to stop fighting and flailing. Ask for help, and be open to doing what it takes to help yourself.

His assistance and rescue can be practical (e.g., frozen lasagna from a neighbor, reference to a therapist) and unconventional ways (e.g., random advice from a stranger or an out-of-the-blue solution).

He can contact us if we are open and clearing the landing area for His metaphorical helicopter. His rescue is firm and sets our feet back on solid ground.

I've experienced the enormity of this kind of grief. It was crushing. The soil of life as I knew it crumbled around me, and the following days were a blur. While the collective memory from those days may be a blur, the pain from each flash remains clear.

If you're in that place today, wondering if you'll ever break free, please let me share some clarity from the other side of my experience. I was sinking in those early days of loss, but I was never sunk. That's quite an important distinction I want to convey.

There were certainly days when I felt as if my sadness was almost too much to bear. I look back on those days, and I can see that I had a framework present all along, which kept me from sinking into grief. But I couldn't see it on those days because I was flailing in fear. The fear was not preventing me from seeing this framework. It was the flailing that blocked my view.

I had solid ground under me all along, even on the days when I didn't realize it. The debris of each loss wrapped around my legs like quicksand. I couldn't feel the bottom, but God provided support and my pathway to the edge, where solid ground awaited.

What framework keeps our head above the water when the wind and rains of hard times beat down on us?

"Everyone then who hears these words of mine and does them will be like a wise man who built his house on the rock. And the rain fell, the floods came, and the winds blew and beat on that house, but it did not fall because it had been founded on the rock. And everyone who hears these words of mine and does not do them will be like a foolish man who built his house on the sand. And the rain fell, and the floods came, and the winds blew and beat against that house, and it fell, and great was the fall of it."

Matthew 7: 24-27 ESV

In the story above, Jesus tells us the importance of building our lives on solid ground. Jesus is the solid ground. Whether we realize it or not, we're all building our metaphorical house on something, be that material wealth, fame, success, being loved, a career, our kids—the list can go on and on. When life is going along smoothly and comfortably, these foundations might suffice. The cracks or lack of supply can hide in the framework on which we've built our lives. But when a hurricane or surprise storm blows through, we discover a house of cards, now fallen.

Gentle breezes and sweet times are comforting and worth celebrating, but they can also bring a false sense of security to those living in a house on sand. When torrents of rain and violent winds of loss and grief hit, the shortcomings in their life framework become apparent, and the crash can be devastating.

Building our life on solid ground, that is, on Jesus and what He has done for us, is the only anchor that keeps us tethered to His strength and peace in the middle of a storm.

The rock in life that will withstand every storm is made of knowing that God is real, that Jesus died for us to make us whole, and that we can choose to accept these truths. He will always be big enough for us to stand on. Our heads are never underwater.

TRY THIS: SCRIPTURE LIFE APPLICATION

Consider the Scripture below, one of my favorites to read when I feel myself heading towards a plot of sinking sand, especially when I feel fear rising.

> *"God is our refuge and strength, an ever-present help in trouble. Therefore, we will not fear, through the earth give way and the mountains fall into the heart of the sea, though its waters roar and foam and the mountains quake with their surging."*
>
> Psalm 46:1-2 NIV

Grief has a way of pulling the ground out from under our feet. We can feel as if the mountains of security or safety that we've built around us are falling into the roaring and churning sea of heartbreak.

There's only so much a broken heart can absorb, and just as an oversaturated hillside comes loose, slipping away from its foundation, grief can feel like a muddy, sticky, scary trap. The Scripture above gives us the promise that God is our shelter and strength, always present to help, no matter what trouble we find ourselves in.

No matter how hard this time feels or how overwhelming today is, we have an ever-present helper."

- Read the Scripture for today three times, aloud if possible. Personalize it by replacing your own name:
- Write this verse in your journal or on a notecard to remember.
- Take a moment to pray about what the verse is teaching you about where you find yourself.
- Think about how this Scripture applies to you.
- A question to ponder: is faith in God a rock for you now, or do you feel the sinking sand?

God is (your name)'s refuge and strength, and ever-present help in trouble. Therefore, (your name) will not fear, though the earth gives way and the mountains fall into the heart of the sea, though its waters roar and foam and the mountains quake with their surging.

SIXTEEN
FINDING THE SOLID GROUND

"Cast your cares on the LORD and he will sustain you, He will never let the righteous fall."

Psalm 55:22 NIV

Yesterday, we considered sinking sand a metaphor for going through trials without a life built on the rock of faith in Jesus. Today, we're going to dig deeper into that element of faith.

This walk through life is full of ups and downs and times of confusion or disappointment. God stands nearby, encouraging us to look His way. He has a plan for our lives and designed us for a particular destiny. We're wired inside with the gifts and personality required to grow into the person we are fashioned to be. There's only one thing missing from our internal core: a critical element that makes us whole.

The realization that God is real and can be known personally can come at any point in a person's life journey. For me, it happened at age sixteen.

I remember that week with a sharp clarity. The college where my dad taught held a special event for students and faculty—the first night of the week-long event featured a teaching that was powerful and compelling. I felt a deep tug at my heart to respond and accept Christ as my Savior, but I ignored the feeling and refused the request. I was afraid to do it.

I argued with my dad the second evening, refusing to return to the next meeting. I was determined and stomped up the stairs to run the water for a bath. That's when it happened.

As I turned on the faucet, still fuming in youthful determination to be right, I was stopped in my tracks when I heard a soft voice interrupt my thoughts,

"Janet, if you were to die tonight, I don't know you."

This changed everything and rearranged me deeply. This voice was God inviting me to know Him. I never finished the bath that night because I had a critical decision: asking Jesus into my life. I've never been the same since.

The life-altering decision to accept the truth of God's love and desire to know us personally comes in as many different avenues as people. My husband, George, came to an understanding and decided to accept Christ as more of a dawning. He described it as the sun rising in his understanding, which was powerful but took time.

Your experience of knowing God is yours; mine is no more real or impactful. My decision as a sixteen-year-old was put in place to steady me and be the rock and spiritual foundation that would be called upon to withstand the storms in my life, which I had no way of knowing were up ahead for me.

The solid ground I've discovered in building a faith that holds me up when sinking-sand days appear. During trials that make no sense, peace, and confidence fill my limited understanding when I put my trust in God.

My prayer for you is that you choose to have this, too. It's as easy as saying "yes" to God, who is calling your name too.

TRY THIS: MY FAITH JOURNEY

No matter where you are in your faith walk, it's helpful to tell the story of it, even if it's only to yourself. It's easy to forget where we started or when the seed of faith was planted. You may feel like the solid ground of God in your life now is only the size of your shoe print. Others may be able to look back and see a long and wide swath of spiritual growth.

Or maybe you've not started your personal journey of faith, but you're still searching for the answers you know are out there. No matter what, a story always has a beginning, a middle, and an ending. The wonderful thing about having a relationship with God our Father is that our ending is heavenly.

Let's journal.

- If you have a faith story or journey to tell, write it out. It's a good reminder to remember God's faithfulness, especially when facing hard days.
- If you've not yet confronted the choice to know God, write about that. He loves you more than we can understand and is waiting to have you turn your heart towards Him. He wants to hear your questions and your fears about the place where your understanding of Him is right now. Write about it.

Here are some questions to prompt your writing, or ask your own question to write about:

- My journey into faith in God started when…
- My understanding of who God is…
- I can see God's hand on my life when…
- I met Jesus in a personal way when…

- If my choice to know God (or not) had its own voice, it would say…

SEVENTEEN
THE SOLO PILGRIMAGE

"We must accept finite disappointment, but never lose infinite hope."

Martin Luther King Jr

ACCEPTING THE WAY THINGS ARE, especially after a loss or heartbreak, takes time and is hard. There's no way around that fact.

Even the insignificant things can't escape the need to accept things now. An example from grieving my son's loss was that it took more time than I anticipated not to mindlessly grab an extra placemat when setting the table for dinner after he died. The reminders of loss, like his empty spot at our family's table, are inevitable shards of pain. Life is simply no longer as it was, even at the dinner table.

For many of us, the meaning of grief will entail learning how to live around the gaping crater left by the loss. We learn where to step to avoid falling into further pain. Of course, knowing how and where to stand safely at the edge takes practice.

In the early days of a fresh loss, standing at the edge of this crater feels like gazing into the top of an erupting volcano. The longer I choose to stand there, the more I can feel red-hot lava of loss bubble up, spitting into my mind, burning pieces of the past. Each memory and unfilled hope or unlived dream leaves my raw heart further blistered.

When I've spoken to others on similar journeys, these early days of deep grief are walked through alone, no matter how many others may intersect with our loss.

Grief is a solo pilgrimage. Accepting the loss is also a unique venture.

For some people, acknowledging the loss is almost as difficult as accepting it. The pain is too big or heavy to put into words. If the grief is carried around without a healthy outlet, we cannot move forward into the new life rearranging itself.

Grief can live alone for a while but will leak out unexpectedly. Depression, anger, isolation, prolonged inability to focus, or bitterly gripping onto the old normal—these are all signs of grief seeping out, whether we like it or not. When we find ourselves in this place and can't seem to move ahead, it's easiest to start by taking small steps. For instance, during the early days of my grief, getting to the next meal was all I could do.

Life goes on, hard as it may seem, and a new normal eventually emerges. The lava cools. Brand-new pieces of life are planted around the edge of the crater of loss. The crater that once left blisters now blooms with flora and fauna we've never imagined.

As we take these intentionally small steps, new routines, new coworkers or friends, new places to live, new physical limitations, and new choices or attitudes will fall into place. Things will shake out, and the additions can be seen as God's way of settling you into a fresh space and a new purpose.

For me, the void that one companion left is filled with multiple, each who enriched my life differently. My husband isn't forgotten or diminished, but his passing has allowed me to expand my life with flourishing friendships that I might not have acquired otherwise. Instead of a husband to spend the evening with, I have a new posse of women friends. We find togetherness despite our aloneness in life. We band together for meals, support, wine-drinking, and shared chores.

Even with a crater of loss, accepting life as it is now takes time and courage to keep going. New and different may not necessarily be considered "better," but with time, the new growth will find its fit.

TRY THIS: A NEW WAY FOR AN OLD THING

Do one of your daily habits, tasks, or rituals today, but do it differently. For instance:

- If you always eat with friends in a restaurant but have never eaten alone in a restaurant, pick a place for a meal and bring a book or magazine to read.
- If you always drive to a specific destination, try taking Uber, public transportation, or the scenic route.
- If you always make your bed, try not making it or make it in a different order.
- Pick a new one if you always listen to the same radio station while preparing for the day.
- If you always take a shower, try a bubble bath.
- Or use one of your ideas from Week 2, Day 5!

After you've done your daily thing in a new way, jot down how it felt and how those sensations might compare to your experience of adjusting to a new normal. Then, be proud of yourself for trying something new.

Today I...

EIGHTEEN
REBUILDING & LEARNING TO ACCEPT

"True life is lived when tiny changes occur."

Leo Tolstoy

THE SCRAPS and blown-out windows left behind from a loss of major destruction require rebuilding plank by plank, many times rebuilding into something entirely new.

Reconstructing your world after any kind of loss or devastating change is a weighty undertaking, but eventually, it's a task everyone is called upon to do at least once. The first steps often go unnoticed by the casual observer because the initial phase of post-loss reconstruction begins with internal adjustment. There are countless ways that internal adjustments occur during the grieving process. Here are three examples:

Forgiveness

Forgiveness is one of the obvious and often seemingly insurmountable internal adjustments. What is important to acknowledge is that forgiveness is a choice. This choice does not require anyone else to know we've made it. Forgiveness is for you, not for the offender.

This is important to understand, particularly for those of us grieving. Forgiveness requires zero fanfare, and no parade is necessary. It can be a choice that is made more than once, a choice made many times over.

Forgiveness takes a conscious effort, especially if the offending party doesn't deserve the forgiveness. However, once made, forgiveness can free a relationship and you from past struggles. Forgiveness on its own may not do the relationship-rebuilding, but it lets go of feelings of resentment or bitterness and justified hurt. To forgive takes a heart change.

"Out of the depths I cry to you, O LORD; O LORD, hear my voice. Let your ears be attentive to my cry for mercy. If you, O LORD, kept a record of sins, O LORD, who could stand? But with You there is forgiveness."

Psalm 130:1-4 NIV

We can choose in our mind, all day long, to forgive, and unless we decide to let the Holy Spirit heal the wound and pour the oil of restoration over us, we can't be completely free. Christ forgives us, so with Him, we can forgive others. Sounds easy, but the mercy we show others comes from the mercy God has shown us to forgive our sins.

Letting Go

When faced with any task, no matter the size, I normally finish big projects one small piece at a time. But it took me years after my little boy died until I felt ready to unpack the dresser drawers of his clothes. The day finally came when I could fold up his clothes and put them in donation bags. As his mom, every shirt and sock was known to me, and every item was very personal.

It seemed like the final goodbye. Some might see donation bags as a small step, but this leap helped me move on. My grieving process added layers of strength that built over time until one day, I realized "it was time."

The additional beauty of this internal shift was that the emotional significance of my son's loss moved to a new part of my heart. The small act gave rest to areas of my heart, too tired from grieving. The shift built a bridge across my broken heart so I could walk to other uncharted pieces of grief. With every internal shift, I found new meaning to each loss. This has been one of the keys to my rebuilding process. I pick up a shard of my grief and give it a new meaning. You might find your rebuilding process to be similar.

Loss and heartbreak don't always make sense. We have every right to be devastated and mad. Sadness feels heavy and overwhelming. There are some things, especially painful things, that we won't know the reason or purpose for their happening. Period, we'll never know.

Learning to Accept

God will use these mysterious circumstances to test our faith and give us the opportunity to trust Him more profoundly. Something shifts in our spirit when we cry out that we don't understand. At that point, we don't even have to accept our circumstances fully because God can work with you from wherever you are, even if you're simply willing to learn to accept. When we lay down the fight to reconcile our new circumstances, we can be filled with peace inside the storm.

God picks us up and holds us, whispering His strength into our shattered life. That's the miracle, and that's when the rebuilding starts.

TRY THIS: WRITE A NOTE

Often, rebuilding starts with a reconnection with someone who is/was important to you.

- Who has helped you make one of these three internal adjustments? (forgiveness, letting go, and learning to accept)
- Write a note to that someone, preferably via snail mail. It could be a simple postcard or a note. Try not to email or text. There's

a benefit in the added intention of handwritten communication.
- In your note, simply thank the person for helping you rebuild your life, even in a small way. Specifics aren't necessary unless you'd like to share them.

Hopefully, sharing your gratitude will make their day (and yours) a little sunnier. Let's celebrate that life is a gift and that the sun rises even when we don't notice, even on cloudy days.

NINETEEN
THE SUN ALSO RISES

"Even the darkest night will end and the sun will rise."

Victor Hugo

I ALWAYS NOTICE A GLOOMY DAY. Sometimes, I welcome them like a blanket wrapped around my shoulders. Dark afternoons, home with my knitting or a new magazine to thumb through, is somehow comforting. I would feel guilty if it was a beautiful sunny day, sitting inside accomplishing little, but a gloomy day, especially a cold, gloomy day, seems to call my name to stay inside and curl up. I appreciate that every once in a while.

However, I've had dreary days, even when the sun blazed brightly overhead, and I'm sure you have too. Sadness covers the most brilliant day with internal storm clouds that are dark and full of tears. Grief is a master at settling inside, whipping up thunderclouds of sadness and shooting pain straight to the heart and the stomach. Living inside sorrow is a heavy coat to wear.

However, there will come a time when you realize the cloak of sadness has become lighter, and you are building a new normal, no matter how small the change is. Even feeling impatient and frustrated with your cloak of sadness is a start to moving towards a new normal.

I had a friend who, when a Marine in boot camp, described the way he survived as by setting a goal to make it to the next meal. He knew if he could make it to breakfast, that was a victory. If he could make it until lunch, the day was moving along. Once he made it to dinner, he achieved another day.

I've often thought about his survival tactic during my grief. It made perfect sense to me. Small benchmarks that keep one looking ahead, moving forward, and making a pathway toward the future.

The sun showing up every day is one of the many blessings we can count on. We don't even think about it; it's a given. Period.

I take so much for granted. As I've aged, my parents passed away, and I've started losing friends to cancer or other illnesses. My siblings are all looking at retirement age. Change is everywhere right before our eyes, slipping silently around corners we don't notice.

Moving forward into change can be a trial we put ourselves through, like my friend in boot camp, or it can soundlessly unfold as we carry on and take one day at a time. Either way, the days we are given are a gift.

I remember my dad saying that when we are born, our time clock is wound with the number of days we are to have. Some are given only nine years, like my little boy. Others are given decades into their 90s. If my dad's saying was correct, we each have time to make a difference in this world and fulfill our destiny. The sun rises in our lives, but it also sets. Take hold of the life you have now, no matter how it's changed. Our days have a purpose, realize your new destination and embrace it. Start today.

TRY THIS: LOOK FOR JOY

No matter where you find yourself in the rebuilding process of your broken life, choose today to give yourself a treat. The goal is to practice a new method filled with enjoyment that your reconstruction can produce.

Some ideas might be:

- Bake some cookies.
- Wear a pair of fun socks.
- Plan to fill your table with friends and an easy pasta supper.
- Go to an unexpected gym or dance class.
- Take an extra 15 minutes to buy that game you're eyeing.
- Go to a wine shop for a mid-week tasting and get a favorite bottle for home.
- Buy yourself a bouquet of flowers at the grocery store.
- Get carryout for dinner and have it delivered.
- Find a music jam with a local community meetup group.
- Take an adventure to a used bookstore to find a treasure
- Attend a local open mic just to watch and support a budding performer.
- Take the afternoon to go to a museum or go fishing or hiking
- Go to a local dog park and bring some treats!
- Peruse a yarn shop to give yourself a sensory treat and get inspired by all the colors!
- Bless yourself so you can bless someone else.

TWENTY
LIFTING YOUR EYES

"I lift up my eyes to the mountains—where does my help come from? My help comes from the Lord, the Maker of heaven and earth."

Psalm 121:1-2 NIV

IN THE MIDDLE of a devastating season, I get angry at the circumstances that have an ugly grip on my life. I've been thrown to the ground while the boots of pain marched across my heart. I'm sure you know what I'm talking about.

Circumstances can swirl around us with gale force, all the while whispering in our ears that loss will never change. It can certainly feel that way. The transition that brings a new reality takes time to be absorbed into the cavities it creates.

A while back, my sister was a patient in the ICU. I remember the hours in the waiting room as her body came to terms with its medical crisis. During my visits, I noticed how grief was everywhere throughout the ICU, not only from the patients who were fighting for their healing but also from the family members who took watch beside them.

One particularly large family had gathered for another patient. Their deep, brokenhearted cries told the rest of the waiting room that they had just received devastating news. Their anguish bounced off the walls. Everyone in the room could feel the pain tear through the fabric of their souls. I recall thinking, "I understand this kind of pain. It hit hard in my life, too."

That kind of reaction is a release of unspeakable pain. It's the sound of a family beginning a grief journey that will mark them for life. I don't know which family member they lost, but instantly life can become a dark, sorrowful place. You may be in that place now or have at least passed through its lanes.

When surrounded by loss, there will come a time when looking up and raising your eyes is the only way to start healing.

As followers of Christ and His goodness, we know in our darkest days that we aren't alone. I've been known to cry out the one-word prayer of "Help!". His ears are tuned to His children; as His sheep, we know our shepherd's voice. Our decision to know Jesus in a personal way is the decision that makes all the difference in keeping walking through the darkest days. I encourage you to look up, both literally and figuratively.

If the horizon is where the earth meets the sky, we can raise our gaze to look ahead and avoid the tunnel vision that loss can create. Looking ahead is also a driving tip that avoids a collision. Our attention must be directed ahead, down the road, and not just focused on the car directly in front of us. Looking forward and up ahead keeps us alert to circumstances that need our attention or a new thing our loss wants us to pick up. With this new vision, we find where our future meets the path forward. The horizon is the place of sunrises and sunsets. God paints the sky with glorious colors to remind us of His love and caring.

"But you O Lord are a shield about me, my glory, and the lifter of my head. I cried aloud to the Lord, and He answered me from His holy hill."

Psalm 3:3-4 ESV

That provides an opportunity for us to trust our Lord, which can become a source of strength. Lifting our heads to seek God changes our constant gaze away from the heavy boots of our circumstances and onto Him.

> *"I lift my eyes to the hills, from where does my help come from? My help comes from the Lord, who made heaven and earth."*
>
> Psalm 121:1-2 NIV

TRY THIS: NOTICE THE SKY

If you're able, take a short walk to let your heart and mind breathe in the depth and beauty of the sky. Make a point to look up, literally and figuratively, so that you can really see the clouds, their formation, and color.

Take a few deep breaths, and thank God for who He is and the plan for your life now, even if you don't know it, no matter how different it may seem.

Today, your challenge is to do one of two things:

Write:

- *If you're outside*, write what the sky or air around you feels like. Set a timer for 8 minutes and use as many descriptive words as possible. Complete sentences are not necessary.
- *If you're indoors*, write what the air and environment around you feel like. Set a timer for 8 minutes and use as many descriptive words as possible. Complete sentences are not necessary.

Draw:

- *Use your available tools* (does not have to be fancy) to sketch the sky as you see it. Be sure to include elements communicating how the sky makes you feel now. Set a timer for 8 minutes and see what unfolds.

Remember that the sky's brilliance is a promise; your days ahead hold purpose.

TWENTY-ONE
FINDING STABILITY AFTER CHANGE (RECIPE: DIJON MUSTARD SALAD DRESSING)

"Every valley shall be filled in, every mountain and hill made low. The crooked roads shall become straight, the rough ways smooth."

Luke 3:5 NIV

SPIRITUAL & Life Emulsifiers

Many of the principles in Scripture are contradictions. How can our place of weakness be made into strength? When the Apostle Paul complained of an affliction that he considered "a thorn in the flesh," the Lord responded by explaining to him,

"My grace is sufficient for you, for my power is made perfect in weakness."

2 Corinthians 12:9 NIV

I think of perfection and weakness as working spiritually like oil and water -- each a separate characteristic. Many think they aren't compatible, but they *can* actually function together and enhance each other, only in certain circumstances. As with oil and water, if an emulsifier is in the mix (also known as a stabilizer), these two can blend into a harmonious outcome.

Perfection and weakness can complement each other during circumstances that call for God, grief, forgiveness, tragedy, fear, humility, confusion, and so on.

Change in life is the symbolic "whisking together," which allows God's perfection and our imperfection to cling to one another. The same goes for oils and water in the kitchen.

God is a master at taking a situation where our human strength or ability is lacking and pouring into us His divine power. We are given the grace, mercy, and strength to withstand an impossible circumstance.

Eventually, becoming a "party of one" caused me to let go of things in my life that at one time blended well with when my husband was alive or when my daughter lived at home.

For instance, I have no use for my husband's "man-cave" fly-fishing magazine stack. He was passionate about developing and tying the perfect bait for rainbow trout, but I only liked to eat the trout, not catch them. The magazines had their purpose at one time, but now are easy to remove.

His essence still hangs in the air, but now I can see more light in my basement, a must-have to see the sky and keep my focus up. I've found it important to keep my literal chin up as much as possible during grief. It's as if I get a psychological benefit from not gazing down. I've noticed that the more I keep my head bent and eyes downcast, the more this keeps my spirits low.

We were created to be in community with others and have contact with others; this includes eye contact. It's in our God-given nature.

Even as a toddler, my grandson always takes it upon himself to seek out people and have them look at him. He stares, smiles, waves, says "hi," and acts charming in every way possible just to get someone's attention. He treats the grocery cart as his chariot to connect with fellow shoppers, bringing joy and looking up wherever he goes. I've tried to follow the lead of this darling 2-year-old because I think he's onto something. Being alert and aware of other people around me, giving a smile or a "good morning" greeting to a stranger, somehow lifts my spirits, too. Look up and see who and what's around you. You can be a blessing too.

Strength from My Weakness

This week's chapter heading, **Creating Stability After Change,** has given us a chance to examine how we reshape our world. We can stand on the solid ground Christ makes for us, no matter how soggy life gets. He helps us accept how life is now, showing us how to rebuild with a new purpose.

TRY THIS: A RECIPE — DIJON MUSTARD SALAD DRESSING

This week, I've selected a recipe that takes two incompatible liquids, then blends and stabilizes this blend by adding one additional agent.

These ingredients don't naturally don't mix but work beautifully together given the right ingredients and circumstances. As oil and water don't naturally combine, the Lord delights in fusing our weakness with His strength to demonstrate His love for us.

In preparing oil-based salad dressing using olive oil and vinegar, an emulsifying agent is necessary to cause blending, creating a silky smooth dressing. Dijon mustard is the emulsifying agent in our recipe. As mentioned, emulsifiers break down the molecules and allow two incompatible liquids to merge.

Grab a bag of fresh salad greens and make a lovely homemade salad dressing. As you enjoy the spicy bite, remember how two seemingly incompatible items can be used together if there is an agent to bring them together. God is in your mix, and He will break down your weakness and fill it with His strength.

This classic, simple, quick salad dressing will make your greens happy. Making homemade salad dressing is easy and worth the 5-minute effort. Especially if you are a *vinaigrette-dressing* person, you may never go back to store-bought.

Enjoy your salad!

Dijon Mustard Salad Dressing

Ingredients:

- ⅓ cup olive oil
- 1 tablespoon of lemon juice
- 1 tablespoon of red wine, white wine, or sherry vinegar
- 1 clove of garlic, minced (optional)
- Salt and pepper

Directions:

1. Add all ingredients to a small bowl and whisk together. Even simpler, add all to a small jar, add the lid, and shake. That's IT!
2. Grab a bag of lettuce mix, toss it with dressing, and dig in!

WEEK FOUR: FINDING MEANING IN A NEW PATH

"See I am doing a new thing! Now it springs up; do you not perceive it? I am making a way in the desert and streams in the wasteland."

Zechariah 4:10 NLT

TWENTY-TWO
TAKING EXITS & NEW OPPORTUNITIES

"We're not lost. We're just headed somewhere different."

~ Emily X.R.Pan, *The Astonishing Color After*

THERE ARE times on a journey when taking a different route or turning around is necessary. In these moments I'm reminded that exit ramps have a purpose and can be as important as any entrance or on-ramp. They can lead us to safety in an emergency fire alarm. They are a traveler's smooth transition in a new direction. An exit always ushers in another entrance.

Life is full of exits; we graduate to new levels in school, we leave home to work out our destiny, we leave singlehood for marriage, we change jobs or careers, we move to new states, our health takes a turn, and loved ones revolve in and out of our lives. Each of these exits, plus many others, opens new doors to walk down hallways of unknown passage.

I had no way of knowing the detours that my life would encounter. Each exit took me to corners I didn't know how to navigate. Circumstances beyond my control pushed my life into directions I never planned to go. It was as if my highway had ended abruptly and unexpectedly. I didn't want to exit or take a detour; I felt I had no choice.

However, it's been said there is always a choice to be made, even when something seems impossible. Often, the choice is how we respond or react to an impossible circumstance, especially one that changes our life. For example, I wish my son and husband hadn't died, and I want my daughter and her family to live closer to me. I want to hold onto things that are slipping through my fingers. But circumstances often don't unfold as we would like. Life is full of departures of things familiar and loved. New corridors appear that change direction and provide a different path to walk. It takes courage to step out, not knowing what lies ahead.

My choice, and possibly yours as well, is to see the exit ramps up ahead and slow down to take them at a safe speed. There might be patches of black ice of disappointment or wild curves we can't see around the bend. We just need to hold on to the wheel and keep going. Scripture tells us,

> *"If the LORD delights in a man's way, he makes his steps firm; though he stumbles, he will not fall, for the LORD upholds him with his hand."*
>
> Psalm 37:23 NIV

In this Psalm, David explains that for those of us who have committed our ways to the Lord and trust Him, God delights in us and will protect us and give us the direction we need. It's all about keeping our surrendered focus on Him.

God provides comfort when we are facing the unknown. Scripture also tells us:

> *"Trust in the Lord with all your heart and lean not on your own understanding; in all your ways submit to Him, and He will make your paths straight."*
>
> Proverbs 3:5-6 NIV

Life's path can get very crooked, with twists and turns we can't predict or see around. When facing the unknown, we often don't have the understanding to know what is up ahead, so we trust the One who can make our path straight, even if we don't understand.

We don't need to be afraid of any exit ramp that shows up in life. God has the map and will guide us to new places. We can learn how to assume new roles and limitations, make new memories, and even find contentment in being alone. It's our choice to keep our eyes on the one who holds the steering wheel.

The losses I've experienced have allowed me to grow in faith and courage just by walking down the exit ramps I faced. Losing my son, then my husband, and my daughter leaving home, all of a sudden, I became a household of one. In my first book, *Hello Nobody, Standing at the Door Alone, What to Do When Everything Changes*, I explain further how I realized becoming a solo was a new experience in many ways.

I have a twin brother. We jokingly call each other our "womb-mate," so it was a new experience for me to do things alone, even as a child. I remember the day we were split up from the same first-grade classroom. I fell for the explanation from teachers that the other first-grade class needed another female student. I was that one. But fear struck hard when I realized being separated from my brother, I had no way of his helping me. I never learned how to spell our last name for the top of classwork checked at the teacher's desk. I simply copied my brothers' spelling.

I had to come up with a quick excuse for the lack of a surname on my work page. Standing in line at the teacher's desk, waiting my turn, I came up with what I thought was a brilliant solution when asked why only my first name was written on my page. I knew I needed a quick answer, so when asked, I gave my only solution: "I don't have a last name." She didn't buy the excuse, so I missed recess and spent the time writing my last name on the blackboard 25 times.

All that to say, sometimes, when faced with a new, unplanned, or unexpected situation, our best solution isn't always the best route to take.

Exit ramps come in all shapes and sizes. For many years, I owned a yarn shop, called Knitwits. The customers and staff became my community, and the shop was a safe place to land when my husband died.

However, when I sold the shop, I feared that taking this life exit would keep me from spending time with my favorite community members. Instead, I discovered I had more in common with my friends than just knitting.

Another example is when my daughter and her family moved away. I was not looking forward to missing them. But I soon discovered that the long-distance made space for new travel adventures and forced us all to get better at staying connected using technology.

But any kind of change or transition can open up unexpected results. Spelling confidence, deeper friendships, and even the courage to close the door on a business all provide the opportunity to trust that God has our route mapped out, exits and all.

TRY THIS: NOTICE A NEW THING

Even if your grief stems from just one major loss in life, you're likely grieving many aspects of that loss. One rock thrown into a lake can create many splashes and ripples. This activity is a chance to explore the many opportunities that loss opens in your life.

What are ten new things that have emerged from your recent exits? What have you discovered as a result?

FINDING THE MEANING OF GRIEF

Ex: Grieving the loss of __(activity)_____ gave me the opportunity to ___(new activity)_____.

Ex: Grieving the loss of breakfast every morning with my husband gave me the opportunity to have brunch with my gal pals.

1. Grieving the loss of _____ gave me the opportunity to _____.

2. Grieving the loss of _____ gave me the opportunity to _____.

3. Grieving the loss of _____ gave me the opportunity to _____.

4. Grieving the loss of _____ gave me the opportunity to _____.

5. Grieving the loss of _____ gave me the opportunity to _____.

6. Grieving the loss of _____ gave me the opportunity to _____.

7. Grieving the loss of _____ gave me the opportunity to _____.

8. Grieving the loss of _____ gave me the opportunity to _____.

9. Grieving the loss of _____ gave me the opportunity to _____.

10. Grieving the loss of _____ gave me the opportunity to _____.

11. Grieving the loss of _____ gave me the opportunity to _____.

Fill in the blanks above, or use your journal to write 10 of your own. If this inspires more writing, go for it!

"See I am doing a new thing! Now it springs up; do you not perceive it? I am making a way in the desert and streams in the wasteland."

Zechariah 4:10 NLT

Take this verse with you and know God is delighted with your progress, no matter how small the footsteps seem. He is making a way for you through this season of pain or confusion. You are exiting to a new place.

TWENTY-THREE
LACE UP THE SHOES

"Blessed are those who mourn, for they shall be comforted"

Matthew 5:4 NIV

I'M NOT A RUNNER. I've jogged a little in the past and did my best time when cars approached, but as soon as they passed, my pace slowed to a walk. I never really had it in me to run. I admire anyone who does, and I always give a silent "You go, girl" or "Way to go" when I drive past someone taking on the task. Not only that, but I wish I were as dedicated and as in shape as they are. You'll notice a runner never runs in flip-flops. Proper shoes are a must.

Footwear is essential for everyone, and it's easily taken for granted. I have a closet full of shoes, ranging from heels I will never wear again and cowboy boots I've only worn once to practical, comfortable lace-ups and favorite worn slippers. Shoes equip us. They offer protection and warmth. We wouldn't be as civilized a society without them.

The grief journey that starts standing at the bottom of what seems like an impossible, ugly mountain to climb requires a different kind of shoe. Trudging through heartbreaking times is painful. Pulling on the proper emotional boots is essential.

No matter what has broken your heart, the road through grief is rocky. It's easy to trip over the stones that litter the path forward. Life may seem fragmented, split between what was before and what is reality now.

These obstacles can be as simple as seeing bananas in the grocery store, a sudden stabbing reminder of how much you miss the loved one who enjoyed the fruit on cereal. Or, as shocking as actually running into the so-called friend your husband is now living with. This sudden stabbing can take our breath away for a moment or two. It's okay to cross to the other side of the street or leave the grocery in tears. Early grief has no right or wrong actions.

As time progresses, the trudge through these days will blend and grow into weeks and months, even years. God's grace to endure can smooth a once-rocky path into a new, familiar pavement. He will outfit your feet with what's necessary to keep going. New ways to do "old" things will become a new normal. God can exchange the heavy, clunky footwear it takes to safely maneuver through the hardest days for a new pair of what's needed. He knows how to custom fit each circumstance for our good and His glory. He's waiting for us to ask for help.

"Then you will call, and the Lord will answer; you will cry for help and He will say: Here am I."

Isaiah 59:9 NIV

Our grief has a beginning, a middle, and an acceptance. The last stage of grief is known as accepting the new normal, the way things are now. It doesn't necessarily mean you are pleased with the reason grief entered your life, but acknowledging the way life is now and making the necessary adjustments is the way forward. There is a strategy to pick up the pieces that have broken off your life and see where they fit into a new reality. My husband helped shape me into the person I am today. His sense of adventure, love of the outdoors, and joy for life were poured into me, and I opened my eyes to see around corners and look for the beauty in simple things. I take all that and fit it into my life now without him. It was born into me by having him in my life. I can carry a legacy of who he was because he gave me the depth I might not have acquired.

Each circumstance is unique and personal, but we can get through it to the other side. The beauty is that there is no rush to reach acceptance. Everyone is on their own timeline. Different "shoes" are required for different seasons. The hikes through my griefs were uniquely mine, as are yours, but we are equipped and furnished with what is necessary to survive the worst days.

> *"I took my troubles to the Lord: I cried out to Him, and he answered my prayer."*
>
> Psalm 120:1 NLT

God has prepared you more than you can know to weather the storm life has thrown you. He uses all time, your past, the present, and the future, to prepare you for such a time as this.

Don't forget to take the important lessons your loss was designed to teach you with you and incorporate them into your new way. Acceptance is building on those lessons to enrich life now. God will empower you to develop the life you have now. Lace up your shoes of God's provision and keep going, one step at a time.

TRY THIS: GRIEF IN SIX WORDS

There's an Ernest Hemingway legend where he gave a challenge to some fellow writers that he could write a story in only six words.

Here is the six-word story Hemingway submitted. Even though the validity of this antidote has been questioned, it still makes a profound statement.

"For sale: Baby shoes. Never worn."

Those six words tell a story so big that a whole picture of grief is painted. A journal prompt to try your hand at is condensing your grief into a sentence of six words.

Hemingway was onto something, suggesting an emotion as overwhelming as grief could fit into such a small space, but you'll be surprised at the power of expressing your grief in a sentence of only six words.

Take some time. It may take a few tries, then write your six-word story in the space below.

_____ _____ _____ _____ _____
_____

TWENTY-FOUR
REST FOR RESTORATION

"But seek first his kingdom and his righteousness, and all these things will be given to you as well."

Matthew 6:33 NIV

God's Word is full of promises to count on, no matter what we face. He knows our needs and specific circumstances. A good father desires to take care of his children. As believers, we are in God's family. Discouragement, fear of the future, physical pain, or sadness are emotions our heavenly Father understands.

He knows that grief is real because He has experienced it first-hand many times. He showed us it's okay to grieve and cry. Furthermore, He knows the pains of heartbreak and disappointment that we encounter.

Jesus is acquainted with grief. Jesus's dear friend, Lazarus, died, and his heart was full of grief and great compassion. This is an example of Jesus's humanity and prompted the shortest verse in the Bible,

"Jesus wept."

John 11:35 NIV

Don't lose the impact of the simple two-word verse. He knew the suffering the mourners felt because he felt it, too.

Jesus was summoned to come when his friend Lazarus was ill, but he didn't arrive for three days. Lazarus' sisters, crushed by his delayed arrival, thought he was too late to make a difference, or so everyone thought.

Jesus showed his love for his friend by sharing his deep human emotion concerning loss, despite his knowledge that Lazarus would become an astonishing show of the miraculous; he was raised from the dead back to life. The full account of this story is in John 11: 1-43.

So much so that after Lazarus' account, Jesus and his disciples withdrew to a region near the wilderness. He has compassion for us not only in our emotional suffering from grief but also when we have physical needs as a result of our grief.

Paul reminds us that God's provision isn't just when we are in pain. He knows every part of us and what we specifically need. One such promise of provision to hold on to reads,

---

"And my God will meet all your needs according to the riches of his glory in Christ Jesus."

Philippians 4:19 NIV

Another promise from Jesus,

> *"Therefore, I tell you, do not worry about your life, what you will eat or drink; or about your body, what you will wear. Is not life more than food and the body more than clothes? Look at the birds of the air; they do not sow or reap or store away in barns, and yet our heavenly Father feeds them. Are you not much more valuable than they?"*
>
> Matthew 6:25-26 NIV

The point for us today is that Jesus knows grief and understands the physical demands of grieving. It can be exhausting, but rest is essential. The body wants to heal from the emotional trauma grief has produced, and the journey to get there requires rest for restoration to begin. Grieving is exhausting work that affects all parts of our mind, body, and soul. Grief's raw, painful side uses tremendous energy inside us and must be built back up. Our bodies cry out for rest, sleep, and relaxation. Allow your body to heal from the inside; rest is necessary for refreshment.

TRY THIS: LOOK FOR REST

Part of God's provision for us is rest. Rest is essential and a component for healing broken hearts. Grief doesn't stop our daily responsibilities. Life moves on, and we are expected to get back into the groove even when our groove is gone.

Rest heals our body inside and out. Needing rest causes irritability and decreases our ability to cope. However, sleep and rest are not the same thing. It's easy to get the two confused. Rest involves restoration. There is such a thing as mental unrest, where our brains are never turned off.

One of many solutions is to keep a notebook at your bedside and write down the things swirling around in your mind. Getting thoughts and concerns on paper is a way to deal with or cope with them at a later time, allowing for much-needed rest and restoration. You can give these thoughts and concerns over to paper.

Look for some rest; take time today to give yourself permission to relax and rest. It does not take up a whole day unless you want it to. Whatever feels restful will be different for you than for someone else.

For example, taking a 10-minute nap in the middle of the day might be difficult for one of my friends, but my late husband had zero problems with this. He purposely brought his lunch to work so that he could shut his office door for an afternoon nap with his feet up on his desk. For him, this was a daily rejuvenation for the remainder of the workday.

My challenge for you today is to pick an item or idea that brings you a sense of rest and can be as simple as you like. Remember that rest is a provision from God that we often don't consider. If you can't come up with what you need for your rest today, ask Him. He knows you better than you do and prompts you with what is required.

Note how you spent your rest here to permit yourself more moments to take a breather. Enjoy.

Make a list of new ways you can enhance your rest and restoration. Please keep in mind that these new ways to rest can add to your meaning of grief.

TODAY, I RESTED BY...

TWENTY-FIVE
SWEET MEDITATIONS (RECIPE: CARAMEL)

> *"Take the first step in faith. You don't need to see the whole staircase, just take the first step."*
>
> Martin Luther King Jr

IF YOU ARE READING this book, something happened to you. It opened the door to a life-altering circumstance; you know what that is. You're living with the change and emotional upheaval it has caused. Even the most common thing might seem raw because of the reordering that took place.

The change you find yourself in now might be part of the healing, or maybe you've been brave enough to step out of an unhealthy circumstance into a fresh start. Perhaps you've been riding the familiar train of life and have been dropped off at an unfamiliar destination with no return ticket. Whatever your story, things will never be the same again. The only thing to do today is to look for the beauty where you find yourself.

You might not be where you want to be right now, but here you are, and nothing can change that.

I have relationships with now dear friends I might never have bumped into had my life not taken the twists and turns it did. I was holding tightly onto how things were before each loss, but when I opened my fist, this allowed my hands to be filled with different things and new people. Furthermore, today, I realize that by moving forward through my grief, I wasn't giving up any part of my loss, nor was I dishonoring those who were missing. Instead, I gained a whole new bouquet.

In this season of life transition and change, we've been given a new post, a new place to stand, a new identity. I went from wife to widow. Maybe you have made the transition from health to chronic pain or illness. Your readjustment may completely depart from a former way of life, employed with security and purpose, to unemployed or forced retirement, where days seem to have no structure. Regardless of your life transition, it's easy to feel as if the place we belong is at the back of the room, unseen by others, making no waves. Many transitions can feel like a spiral going down, to dark and sad tunnels.

But the place we are now isn't necessarily a wrong address. This is the time to rely on the strength God has for each of us so we can see with clear eyes and stand on solid ground among the new scenery all around us. Without His strength, facing the unknown is stressful and emotional enough. Throw grief in the pot, and the mix isn't tasty.

"When I called, you answered me; you greatly emboldened me."

Psalm 138:3 NIV

A promise to count on is that God's ear is bent towards His own, and He makes a new way familiar. He'll give you the strength to do what's before you. This equipping from God can come from people and circumstances placed just at the right time or bend in the road. Be willing to look for these things stationed by God waiting for your notice.

Nothing in this world is permanent. Everything is in continual flux and change. We can grip the things that bring us comfort and security, but even that isn't lasting. One thing we can count on is that nothing remains the same: jobs end, children grow up, parents age, we age, and the stock market fluctuates. Often, the things that seem permanent at the moment slip away as time marches on.

Our vice grips on comfort and security throughout this continual flux can feel like trying to swim across a pool while holding a fistful of sugar. The granules dissolve so quickly and silently through our fingers. The granules have completely changed or vanished when we arrive at the other side.

Sometimes, the things that once brought us comfort are no longer options. The solution? Look around your life and be willing to step out of *what* was into what *is now*. It might feel different and scary out of your comfort zone, but a new thing only needs to be done once, and it's no longer considered a first. This can be as simple as returning to church after a loss alone. I felt as if all eyes were on me, sitting alone without my husband next to me. I was not as noticed in a congregation of over 800 people as I had imagined. Each week, it became easier and easier to walk into church as a single person and find a seat for one.

We have a choice: to constantly stare at the loss and the pain it produces or turn our focus on God, who never changes. Our circumstances shift. He doesn't. That is a comfort we can hold on to when the circle of life seems to be squeezing us into a size that no longer fits.

"I am the LORD; I change Not"

Malachi 3:6 NIV

Grief has a way of altering us. Even small adjustments caused by a loss can bring a hurtful stumble where we feel out of balance and unsteady.

The new people and circumstances that grow from disappointments and heartbreak can bring fresh stability if we choose to see it.

TRY THIS: A SWEET MEDITATION ON CARAMEL

To practice meditating on the promises of change throughout grief, watch or participate in the metamorphosis of something sweet.

Pick your preference from one of the following ways:

1. I've provided a simple recipe to try, or you can find another if you have a favorite for caramel.
2. Find several videos of someone else demonstrating the art of working with sugar + heat to make something new (i.e., search on YouTube for "how to make caramel").
3. Enjoy spending time observing the process of sugar melting into a different physical form. As you notice the changes, consider or read aloud one of the following:

God is a firm foundation in my life*, even when my comfort seems to dissolve or change. He is ready and waiting to steer me through today and all the following days. God will always be there. He will show me how to keep going even in my hardest days.*

God is the firm foundation in my life*. When the familiar things that have brought comfort in the past change, I will be open to seeing the new places and people God will provide for me now. If today's waters are rough and I feel as if I'm sinking, I will remember God is the Way Maker, and He knows the comfort my soul needs.*

Ingredients

- 1 cup brown sugar
- ½ cup butter
- Splash of milk (¼ cup)
- Vanilla, optional

Directions

1. Combine all ingredients
2. Stir over low-medium heat until a slow boil
3. Cook until thick + 1-2 more minutes

It really *is* that simple! Get the ice cream out or add it to your favorite coffee beverage. Tah dah!

TWENTY-SIX
A NEW WAY WITHIN

"True life is lived when tiny changes occur."

Leo Tolstoy

LIFE IS a collection of tiny changes piled on top of each other. These changes lay a foundation to bring about true life. It's my belief, from the Tolstoy quote above, that he understood how life transforms us if we let the small steps take us to our next place.

When a major loss hits our lives, no matter the cause, it's a stomach punch that can take us to our knees. Often, these are moments when God's voice seems the loudest in our ears. Or, it can seem God has no voice and nothing to say to us. His purpose for allowing us to sit for a time when He seems distant is a hard season to understand. We can feel God has abandoned us at our greatest time of need. In Scripture, David certainly gives voice to those feelings,

> *"How long, O Lord? Will you forget me forever? How long will you hide your face from me? How long must I wrestle with my thoughts and every day have sorrow in my heart?"*
>
> Psalm 13:1-2 NIV

Sometimes, it takes the hardest times or darkest days in life to realize God is there, even if we don't think so or feel His presence. God wants us to cry out to him in our pain and suffering in the thick darkness of it. The light of His presence often shines the brightest at our lowest times.

He'll use these hard days to reveal Himself deeper and bigger than ever if we let Him show us where He can be found.

> *"And we know that in all things God works for the good of those who love him, who have been called according to His purpose."*
>
> Romans 8:28 NIV

I've read that verse many times, but it never hit my heart until my life was so profoundly touched by heartache. Suffering is a door that has choices. We can raise a fist to God in anger, stay in despair, blaming Him for not changing an outcome. That approach works for a while but doesn't allow God's grace and peace a place to land. Sure, I was devastated and crushed by my losses, and in those first few weeks of shock, I was angry and confused. But I decided the circumstances were too big, and the hurt was too much to hold.

I remember praying, "Okay, God, I know you see this; I can't handle it alone; I'm not giving into despair, so help me walk through it and see the purpose you will plant through my loss."

A New Way to See Pain & Suffering

Suffering and pain do not indicate that God has forsaken us or isn't there. His promises hold true, no matter what the circumstances look like. Often, our focus is only on our loss and our pain, and this can feel like God's abandonment. During grief, it's easy to think God must not be who He says He is when the truth is that He's even better than we think He is.

We have preconceived ideas or beliefs based on our experiences, past, and unique life stories. However, if your conclusions and beliefs about life are solely based upon your singular perspective, then the framework you're leaning upon for peace and understanding is incomplete. Life is bigger than our pain. We cannot see the big picture for God when we only look through our lived experiences.

James encouraged the early Church to persevere so they would not lack anything. Focusing *only* on pain and suffering ultimately limits our capacity to find peace and understanding in these difficult times. Don't forget that His promises hold true outside ourselves and outside our grief, too.

> *"Consider it pure joy, my brothers, whenever you face trials of many kinds, because you know that the testing of your faith develops perseverance. Perseverance must finish its work so that you may be mature and complete, not lacking anything."*
>
> James 1:2-4 NIV

God works big things into us through suffering and grief. Paul David Tripp wrote one of my favorite books on the subject of suffering. In it, he explains:

> *"That is a remarkable passage [James 1:2-4] because it calls and alerts us to something counterintuitive. We don't typically experience joy in suffering; in fact, many of us lose our joy even in the face of the smallest obstacles. Now, don't misunderstand what James is calling you to here.*

> *He's not saying you should rejoice because of pain and loss. That is not a call to some kind of joyful Christian stoicism. Rather, James is saying that you have reason to rejoice in the middle of your travail because of how God is using your suffering to produce in you what you could never produce in yourself. Suffering in the hands of God is used to fill you up, to grow you up, and to complete God's work in you."*
>
> ~ Paul David Tripp, *Suffering: Gospel, Hope, When Life Doesn't Make Sense*, 2018, p. 180

A New Way in Me & You

God made a new way for me, which started inside my heart. I was given grace and peace to accept seemingly unacceptable circumstances. My faith grew as I realized the courage I was given to take a different path. My relationship with the Lord has grown deeper and more personal as His arms came around me to balance and steady my feet. He gave me strength I didn't think I had within myself.

That was how my New Thing began, and I've never been the same.

> *"See, I am doing a new thing! Now it springs up; do you not perceive it? I am making a way in the desert and streams in the wasteland."*
>
> Isaiah 43:19 NIV

My prayer for you is that as your journey progresses, you see that God can use your pain to draw you closer to Him. It might be the first time you have called out to Him, or you might already have a steady relationship. No matter where you find yourself, His arm is never too short to reach you if you call out to him.

> *"Listen, The LORD's arm is not too weak to save you, nor is his ear too deaf to hear your call."*

Isaiah 59:1 NLT

Think about the new thing your life has unfolded. A new thing doesn't necessarily imply an easy thing. Often, doing something for the first time takes courage and effort. I'm not talking about the bravery it takes to try your hand at sky-diving. Even small things like going to dinner with your couple of friends for the first time as a single, or now having to do all the driving, something a spouse always enjoyed doing, have a new component attached. You may be the only one aware of these "new" things' impact in your life, but they become seeds of growing into your new way.

Unfamiliar things can be a challenge. Remember, once you've done something you've never done, next time won't be the first time. Practice may not make things perfect, but it makes things *easier*.

TRY THIS: TWO WORDS

In your journal or on a notecard, come up with two (2) words:

- **one word** that describes where you are *now* on your road
- **one word** that describes where you want to be in the *future*

Take this to the Lord in prayer and ask Him to speak to you about it. The trick here is that once you ask, you need to be willing to listen to His response. It may be in an impression you get as He nudges you to take an action or a feeling of peace, joy, or forgiveness. Then, watch how these words can teach you.

MY TWO WORDS ARE:

_____

_____

If you like, write your words in the space above as a reminder.

TWENTY-SEVEN
COUNTING DOORS

> *"Look on every exit as being an entrance somewhere else."*
>
> ~ Tom Stoppard, *Rosencrantz & Guildenstern Are Dead*

I ONCE HEARD a sermon that mentioned Scripture's usage of the word "door" and that it was found about 400 times. As I understand the teachings on this subject, the word was often used as a symbolic representation of a given opportunity in life.

There are two ways to consider an open door: an entrance or an exit. A door opens for an entrance in life but also closes as a designed function to provide protection and allow for leaving. Regardless, both usages represent the possibility of a new thing.

The Purpose of Doors

Thinking metaphorically, which doors have opened or shut for you lately? God will use either for the journey you're on now. Every door before us is a decision. It's up to us to take the opportunity offered and walk through whatever potential is waiting. Otherwise, we can know that a closed door has a meaning; we might not understand that meaning in the present moment.

The Cost of Doors

Every door has a cost, which is not necessarily a bad thing. You might be facing a door open to choosing forgiveness. The cost tied to that is bigger than you can know. Even if you've been wronged, asking for and giving forgiveness will free you from the burden of resentment or anger that has been a weight on your back for years. God is in the business of forgiveness and can show you how it works. After all, He's forgiven those who are unworthy and made us His own.

Doors & Decisions

Not every door comes with a clear decision. My friend was recently offered a job she was really excited about. Fortunately, she didn't let her enthusiasm cloud her judgment. As the hiring manager began the onboarding process, it became apparent that the role did not match her or the company well. She sent an awkward but professional email and sadly rescinded her acceptance of the job. Everyone involved was disappointed by the setback, but my friend knew it was the best decision for her and the company seeking the right team member.

Her story is a good reminder that just because a door is open does not always mean it is open for you. Furthermore, if you walk through the wrong open door, sometimes it's best to turn around and retrace your steps. Walking through open doors, wherever they may lead, requires discernment and wisdom.

God can provide insight into purpose only He can see. You can ask God for guidance if you seek more wisdom and discernment about one of your decisions. Every prayer is answered; God hears them all. Many times, the only answers we might hear are a "yes," a "no," or a "not now." If the latter two, this can feel like a closed door. In the case of my friend's job situation, she felt the answer was "not now."

Doors & Their Unknowns

Open *and* closed doors in life come with unknowns. In searching for the meaning of grief, whatever produced our grief will create a door with attached unknowns. When I became a widow, I had no clue what that would feel like or look like practically. It was a door that I walked through after my husband's funeral. I found myself facing an empty house filled with unknowns.

On a lighter note, saying goodbye to single life and getting married is an open door. The arch under which a couple marries is a symbol of this passage to new unknowns. Couples learn about these unknowns by living in a relationship together. No matter how many years you've known a spouse, there are plenty of undiscovered parts to them.

Glimpses Into Unopened Doors

Doors cracked open can be a glimpse of a bigger picture. God gifted me with a reminder of his strength and faithfulness years before my husband died. At the time, I didn't know the depth of insight He was sharing nor how badly I would later need it.

I taught a weekly Bible study with a friend and enjoyed the peaceful drive along the river to get there. I often used the 45-minute drive to pray and spend quietly with the Lord. During this season, my husband was very ill and not getting better.

I remember one day making the drive, pleading in prayer to God, asking for healing, saying that I needed my husband! As soon as I prayed that, a soft voice outside my ear asked, "Why aren't I enough?" This stopped me in my tracks. I felt a deep sense of knowing that God's question to me was also a hint at his answer to my prayer for my husband's healing.

Was God really enough? Could I really trust Him to walk beside me? Even if my prayer for healing didn't happen?

A few years later, when George died, I was reminded of this poignant question. I remember thinking, "I get it now. I know why you asked me that." Throughout the grieving process, weeks and years after my husband's death, I found myself clinging to this same question and its answer. He is enough.

Eight years prior, I had peeked through the door of the cavernous loss that was unfolding before me.

These sudden and soft questions like "Is God really enough?" can crack open our faith so that we can trust God when we need it most. Even if we're scared to ask the questions, God is not scared of them.

Look for the doors that God may have cracked open for you during these days of reordering in your world. He knows what's best for us, even if we think we know better or don't know anything at all.

Whatever door God opens will require you to depend on Him. Whatever door He closes will require you to trust Him that there is something better or a different door at a later time.

TRY THIS: COUNTING DOORS

Take some time to consider the meaning of grief and open or closed doors in your life now in one of the following ways:

- Either go for a walk/drive and notice the doors you pass.
- Or find some photos of doors and sketch out your favorites on whatever paper you have around. (Searching online is a great place for this!)

As you walk, drive, or sketch—consider the following questions:

- What is God teaching you through this imagery?
- Do you see yourself entering through a new door in your life?
- Or are you walking through an exit, closing a door behind you?
- What might be the purpose and consequence of these doors in your life?
- What are the unknowns attached to these doors?

(Psst! These are great journal prompt questions, too.)

TWENTY-EIGHT
FLAVOR PROFILES OF GRIEF (RECIPE: HERB SPRINKLED POPCORN)

"Popcorn is one of the only situations in which you eat the result of an explosion."

Demetri Martin

ADDING flavor to your life *during* grief is perfectly acceptable and often necessary. Grief really *is* awful, especially when we leave out the flavoring and enjoyment that community, joy, color, pets, friends, volunteering, and adventure can add. These are some of the flavor "profiles" that make grief bearable.

Similarly, a dried kernel of corn is practically unedible, but when we add heat, patience, and BAM! Suddenly, you've got one of the most versatile snacks ever.

This week, we've thought about finding meaning in paths that included shoes, rest, open doors, and exits. Here's a review of our days and a new popcorn topping for each. Plus, you'll find my favorite recipe when movie night comes along (or any time!)

Wrong Turns

Life is full of exits and detours, as you know. You may have found yourself at an unfamiliar exit with no map to get you back on the road.

Even traveling with a GPS in my car, I always get lost! I'll end up taking wrong turns as the voice on my phone keeps telling me to "turn around, recalculating…" Once, all of my "wrong turns" landed me in a place called "Hog Holler" in the middle of the Kentucky hills. I knew I was in the wrong place because suddenly, the roads weren't paved, and the air smelled like a pig farm. I was definitely lost, so lost that my GPS couldn't connect to satellites. Fortunately, I was able to call my sister. We laughed about my predicament; she had access to a different map to navigate me back to the highway.

Flavor profile: Life can feel like ending up in "Hog Holler." We have the directions screaming at us, and we still make wrong turns. However, the road eventually straightens out; we call out for help, and it's always there, usually just in time. God has all the provisions we need. Each need is unique to us and understood by Him. Don't leave home without Him.

Popcorn Topping to Try: **Bacon Bits**

New Year's Eve Walk Home

One New Year's Eve, I attended a wedding for my college roommate's daughter. It was a lovely event and blended nicely with the undercurrent of a new year. The venue was out of town, so I secured a hotel room to avoid a late-night drive home. My own daughter was my plus-one date for the evening, which made a fun time even better. The midnight wedding and New Year's Eve balloon drop marked the time to return to the downtown hotel.

I'll never forget that walk. One o'clock in the morning, January 1st, in downtown Columbus, Ohio, is not the time to take your shoes off and walk four city blocks barefoot. It's impossible to get too far down the road if your shoes pinch horribly and give blisters. My feet hurt so badly from the lovely heels I hadn't worn in years. I had to take my shoes off. The only solution was to walk barefoot in freezing temperatures.

Flavor Profile: Life does that to us in many ways. We are hit with an impossible circumstance and left with few solutions. Lace up the 'shoes' God provides to get you through, or take off what doesn't work and trust the sidewalk. Both work to keep going.

Popcorn Topping to Try: Frozen Chocolate Chips

God's Provision or Rest

Rest is more essential than we know. Sleep is a gift of restoration and renewal, and relaxation is a gift to enjoy. Grief can rob us of both rest and relaxation. It's full of exhaustion and often disturbed sleep. On the other hand, grief can cause us to sleep and not want to get out of bed at all. I remember the early days of grief after my son died. I would wake up, open my eyes, and try to determine whether he was really gone or not. Then, the feeling of a boot on my chest taking away my breath, I would remember, 'Yes. He's gone.' I would curl into a ball and wait for the morning tears to stop. Oh, those early days of shocking grief are hard.

Flavor Profile: God does walk beside us, especially when our pain is too big to handle. He's right beside our broken hearts, even when we don't realize it.

Popcorn Topping to Try: Finely shredded cheese & dried cranberries

A New Way

A new way can be a scary way. Even while driving, it's so much easier and more comfortable to drive somewhere you've been before. I've driven to my place in North Carolina for years now, and I'm very comfortable and at ease taking the trip alone. It's something I've done now for years since my husband died.

He was always the driver, and I got accustomed to being the trusting, relaxed passenger. I enjoyed that role and didn't mind how long the drive was. I remember how unsettling it was for me to make the trip alone after he died, even though I had traveled the route for years. Going it alone was different.

Flavor Profile: "Take your time, have practice, and just do it" are the three rules of taking on a new thing today. We can talk ourselves into or out of anything uncomfortable. If not yet, at some point, you will be able to celebrate all the new things this new time in life has opened up for you. It will come, and you will be ready.

Popcorn Topping to Try: Pistachio Nuts

TRY THIS: A RECIPE — HERB SPRINKLED POPCORN

When you are feeling the need for a crunchy snack, and the potato chips were all eaten the night before (or put into a grilled cheese sandwich), reach for this easy salty snack instead. Next to kettle chips, this is a go-to in my house.

I have a large glass microwave popcorn popper. It works perfectly to throw in some kernels and watch it fill with hot, puffy popcorn. For this recipe, the ingredients are basic.

Herb Sprinkled Popcorn

Popcorn Herbs to consider: My favorite is fresh rosemary. This is easy with fresh sprigs of rosemary. Scrape the twig to remove the needles. Before chopping, I like to toast them for a minute in my toaster oven. Chopping the needles to release the flavor also makes a size for popcorn sprinkling.

Other spice blends, like Trader Joe's 21 Seasoning Salute or Herbs de Provence blend, also make savory additions to popcorn. I also love the blend my friend gave me called Crabby Bill's House Blend Spice.

Servings:

Enough to eat alone or share :-)

Ingredients:

- Popcorn popped in any form you like.

- Toasted rosemary (or another dry herb blend)
- Extra virgin olive oil
- Salt and pepper

Directions:

1. Make popcorn your favorite way: stove top, microwave, or popcorn popper.
2. Dump popcorn into a bowl large enough to toss a splash or two of olive oil. This makes the perfect surface for salt, pepper, and herbs to adhere.
3. Mix in rosemary or spices, salt, and black pepper if you like, and there you have it! Be creative; flavor-infused olive oil adds a great touch. There are many to choose from: roasted garlic, Italian herb, truffle, lemon—the selection is huge. Pick up a favorite EVOO and be ready for a popcorn treat!
4. This pairs perfectly with a movie and a glass of something yummy.

WEEK FIVE: FINDING MEANING IN RESTORATION

"We forget that God's primary goal is not changing our situations or relationships so that we can be happy, but change us through our situations and relationships so that we will be holy."

Paul Tripp

TWENTY-NINE
RENEWED STRENGTH

> *"It's your reaction to adversity, not adversity itself, that determines how your life's story will develop."*
>
> Dieter F. Uchtdorf

EACH OF US is stronger than we think. Even as I look back at my weakest place, I can see now that I plowed through tasks I never thought I could handle. I cried a lot, asked for help, and wanted to give up. Some days, I did give up, heading back to bed. But somehow, I managed to climb out of bed and then climb up mountains as I moved through my grief. But I learned an important lesson in doing so. I couldn't do it alone.

I know the same can be true for you, too.

Inner endurance grows taller as we are forced to lean into more than our own strength. On the days we melt into puddles of despair and loneliness, deep down, there is a spark of strength that can be fanned into a flame of courage by God's place in our lives.

No matter how intense or even irrational, these emotions serve a purpose that God does not miss. He hears our whispered prayers and doesn't turn away from our outbursts.

Grief wears us out. It is exhausting at times, emotionally, spiritually, and physically. I remember, in my early days of grief, moving through my day in a zombie-like fashion. It was difficult even to pick a spaghetti sauce brand in the grocery store. I would finally scream in my head, "Just pick one!" I was easily distracted doing simple tasks. I would start a simple chore and get sidetracked in the middle, leaving half unloading the dishwasher or forgetting a load of clean laundry in the washer for a few days. The fog of grief can be frustrating and sap our energy.

There were days when I felt as if I had no strength. It's easy to feel irritable, cranky, and short-tempered when there is emotional depletion. Grief is heavy. It feels oppressive and thick inside our hearts and brains.

When our strength is gone, we must look for it somewhere else. I didn't need any more of my own weakness; I couldn't rely on that. I needed God's strength. He came through in pouring that into my life and used an armful of lovely friends to show me His love.

Society says, "You are enough; your inner strength can get you through anything as long as you believe you can." That works until it doesn't work anymore. Realizing that we really can't do it all, especially alone and especially when in grief, is a very freeing notion. It can change everything, such as giving up your "right" to be strong enough to go through life's challenges all by yourself. Otherwise, our knees can eventually buckle under heavy grief if the load isn't shared. I should know.

I wanted to crawl into a hole when my husband died. My identity as a wife was gone, and I didn't want to be labeled as single. In filling out forms, if there were only two choices to select, single or married, I always wrote in the word "widow." In my mind, I was fighting the battle of a role change, and I wanted my label to be clear. I was trying to fit my former round life into a new square space, and I thought I didn't need any help.

I wanted to be enough, alone, as I came to terms with my singleness. However, what came to be true is that I needed other people who parked themselves around my life. They helped me learn how to live my new life. I didn't know what I didn't know. I see now how God answered my prayer to help me. He sent reinforcements to the community. The trick was that it was there all along, but I needed to accept the offered help. God works through people. He gives assignments to be His hands and feet and show His love.

God's provision may show up in all kinds of ways. There's a purpose in Grief Support Groups, or finding like-minded interest groups like walking or biking, to provide the opportunity to be around other people. Book clubs, church groups, choir practices, gardening groups, knitting groups, classes to take, volunteering to serve food at a shelter—a few ideas to get you thinking about stepping out of your comfort zone, no matter how uncomfortable it has become.

Simply talking *myself* into healing or building strength or becoming happier wasn't going to work. I needed more than *me*; I needed other people, and more than that, I needed to realize God had His hand in my situation all along. This was a turning point in my grief.

The others I let into my grief were a source, a spark to light the flame of my healing, realizing sometimes, God's strength is sent through others.

"Finally, be strong in the Lord and in His mighty power."

Ephesians 6:10 NIV

God can turn us around from our grief and point us in a new direction. But we must let Him and ask for His help. He has a purpose in everything, even our hardest things.

Real strength comes when we give up relying on our own strength and discover how we need more of God and what He can offer and less of ourselves.

Through your circumstances, God can show you how *your* strength, paired with *His* and the resources He sends your way, will enable you to be stronger than you think. You have more resolve than you know and have the ability inside you to keep moving ahead. Our heavenly Father is looking down the road of your life, ready to fill you with the strength necessary for one day at a time.

TRY THIS: PROMISE FOR RENEWED STRENGTH

"He gives strength to the weary and increases the power of the weak. Even youths grow tired and weary, and young men stumble and fall: but those who hope in the Lord will renew their strength. They will soar on wings like eagles; they will run and not grow weary, they will walk and not be faint."

Isaiah 40:29-31 NIV

Use this verse to be encouraged about the new strength you are developing. Take it with you.

Your stamina will be formulated to carry you through, no matter how small it is now. Renew or exchange your broken strength for God's perfect peace; He will empower you to do everything required.

That's His promise. If you like, take a few minutes to journal about:

- The renewed strength you find in your life now. Have you tried anything in particular to rejuvenate something new in your life?
- How does the verse for today encourage the new strength that's developing in you?

- Have new people or places come into focus that have helped you not grow weary?

THIRTY
CATCHING CURVEBALLS

"Life is like riding a bicycle. To keep your balance, you must keep going."

Albert Einstein

CHANGE DOESN'T ALWAYS BRING insight, but it can bring change.

A circumstance, especially one created from a grief event, can be a powerful learning tool. Lessons that mark us deeply are what we discover about ourselves in times of sorrow. I was not prepared to live life alone. Truth be told, as a twin, I was a pair from conception. I always had a playmate, shared birthdays, shared a stroller, and shared a special bond that twins develop. I always had roommates in college and graduate school and married when I finished school. So, learning how to live alone took some time for me. I gained new insight into solo life and have a heart for others who are single. I know what it feels like to be the one who instigates plans to be with other people.

When life throws a curveball and turns things upside-down, understanding seems impossible. Grief has many disjointed parts, and making sense of it can feel like our thoughts are like laundry tumbling around in the dryer. Sadness and the unknown are heavy when damp with fresh loss.

A time comes when insight will grow into your circumstance. The losses in my life were certainly unwanted and uninvited, yet there they were, taunting me to accept the change they dug into my world. I'm still learning to live around the missing pieces and swallow the change. It chokes and can be difficult to accept, but a strength grows from letting go of the way things were. It gives us a place to expand into what is necessary now and carry on into the new reality created by our loss.

However, it can feel like your loss is too big even to consider a new thing. That's okay. Just know those of us a little farther ahead on the road of acceptance have had more time to climb our wall of grief. It doesn't matter where you find yourself on your grief journey or how many days, months, or even years it's taken to get where you are now; you can find rest and emotional restoration. It comes in due time. But we've got to be willing to allow space for new insights, even if we never get an answer to our "why" questions.

Letting go creates space for insight to come in. We're often called to accept a circumstance without fully understanding it or, for that matter, wanting it. *Letting go* of a hard thing doesn't necessarily imply ignoring the hurt or suffering it has caused. The point is opening up our grief spot to accept something new. But just know, this stage of moving on and facing what is now takes time and, often, only by little bites of acceptance at a time. You know the old saying, 'How do you eat an elephant? One bite at a time.' That word picture helped me keep moving into my new future. I could handle a bite and give myself time to swallow it. Loss can be so big, it's all we can do, and that's okay.

Accepting a loss, as in the death of a loved one, a career-ending unexpectedly, or coming to accept any type of ending, is really hard. A choice is made about the new reality. Often, it's difficult to realize how little control we have over the particular circumstance that has produced our grief. No matter how tightly we hold on to what has slipped out of our lives, eventually, we must come to terms with the fact that the particular person, relationship, expectation, or role is now gone. The tighter we clutch our fists in defiance of a loss, the harder it is for our brains to make sense of what has happened. It's been said that acceptance is the hardest part of grieving, and it takes the most time. It's usually one of the last stages of grief if one is keeping score.

The pathway towards insight into what life has become brings renewal. Life can resume, no matter how much it has been changed by loss. Our lives can be renewed, and so can our minds. Our behavior, mood, or choices begin in the mind.

Renewal in any context, whether emotional, physical, or spiritual, is ongoing. Suffering has a way of maturing our faith like nothing else. When life seems to break us, or at least step a crushing boot into our hearts, this raw time can be used by God to show us His presence even in our darkest times. When our world as we know it changes into something unrecognizable, God can plant new things and teach us more profound truths.

Some lessons are best learned from adversity and suffering, and the restoration that comes from those days brings spiritual maturity. Life's insights can grow from heartbreak, as can our relationship with God mature. As God proves Himself to be faithful, no matter what we face, we are given new insight.

"Therefore, we do not lose heart. Though outwardly we are wasting away, yet inwardly we are being renewed day by day."

2 Corinthians 4:16 NIV

Our heavenly Father already has an understanding of our hardest days. He sees up ahead and behind us, all at the same time. It's a comfort to know our journey isn't solo if we have a relationship with the one who sees it all. Ask for insight into what needs to be dealt with now or where to plant your feet.

The place you find yourself now in your grief journey comes from many factors about you and how you are wired to accept or handle tribulations in life.

You have your own theory about grief, realize it or not. Once you figure out your personal theory, the insight will give perspective and help you understand how to travel grief's course.

There is no right or wrong way to feel about grieving.

TRY THIS: HAVE INSIGHT?

Grief has a way of shaking up our world; at times, it is so demanding we don't recognize it—today, journal about your insights.

- Are you comfortable talking about hard or hurtful things, or is it easier to keep these feelings inside yourself?
- Do you consider grief a hurdle you must endure or an obstacle in your way?
- Do you see your grief circumstance as unacceptable, causing anger or hostility?
- Is there some level of peace and acceptance for your particular loss?
- If your grief was a mode of transportation (any mode of transportation!), which mode would describe your current journey the most accurately? Why?

Sometimes, considering a metaphor will help pinpoint how grief works for you. A metaphor is a word picture that is a comparison of two things, often not related. It's a way to give an understanding of a more profound meaning.

For example, is grief more like scaling a mountain or being thrust onto a raft in whitewater with no oar?

Does grief feel as excruciating and sharp as labor pain, giving birth, or floating above your life as on a hot air balloon, passing over what you know but not being part of it?

Realizing a figure of speech that rings true can give perspective to your feelings. Once deciphering the truth in a metaphor, no matter how small, insight can start clarifying life as it is now. (This is also an excellent journaling and creative writing prompt!)

What new things have you seen or gained insight into along your grief journey? Make a list of four insights, no matter how small or angry, and pick one to write about today. Put your pen to paper and start writing. Don't read your words as you go; just let them flow.

Write until you stop. It can be one word or three pages.

GRIEVING HAS TAUGHT ME...
1.
2.
3.
4.

THIRTY-ONE
NAVIGATING A NEW BOAT

"We must row in whatever boat we find ourselves in." ~

Christie Watson

I'VE NOT SPENT much time on a sailboat. However, my extremely limited time *has* taught me that no matter the size or the type of sailboat, it takes a high level of skill to read the wind, hoist the sails, and keep the boat on course.

If you ever have the opportunity to sail, I recommend it! It's thrilling to fly across smooth waters with only an unseen force-filling fabric designed for motion and speed. There's beauty in obeying the captain to duck your head lower when the sails are called upon to "come about" and move quickly to the other side of the boat when the wind suddenly changes. Every command's purpose is to sail properly; each command must be obeyed.

Navigating a New Boat

During grief, we find ourselves sailing a new boat. Grief sits us down in places we have no knowledge or skill to maneuver through until we start moving ahead. At first, grief feels like a heavy wooden row boat with only one oar. We can't paddle a straight line no matter how hard we try. Most days, it feels like all we can accomplish are circles.

Time smooths out our navigation as we exchange a boat traveling in confusing circles for a smaller vessel, a dinghy, small enough to get our bearings and chart a new path. Over time, the boat of our life becomes large enough to accommodate more people, and we are brave enough to travel to new destinations.

I'll Take The Check

Early on the grief journey, it's sometimes difficult to know when or what will kick open the pain and halt us in our tracks. This happened to me on the first New Year's Eve after my husband died; I was persuaded to join our tribe of best friend couples for an evening out to dinner. I was reluctant to go, but I loved these friends and knew they missed George also, so I included myself in their plans.

I had no idea how hard it would be. Seeing an empty seat at the table only made me want to leave. I made it through the meal without my friends realizing how much pain I was in or how lonely I felt. I was alone at a table meant for couples.

Grief took a dive when the checks arrived, and the husbands reached for their wallets. I was left to pay for my solo dinner and quickly exited before walking to my car alone. I cried all the way home. It's such an easy thing now, but it felt like a huge lump in my throat at the time.

Recalling that evening is visceral and sharp in my memory, as are all other "firsts" throughout the grieving process. That evening, I learned some situations would require growing more slowly than others.

Jesus is in the Storms

A solid foundation of God and the inner peace He provides can carry us through no matter what life brings up. A story in scripture gives an account of Peter having faith and courage in the middle of a storm to come to Jesus. They saw Jesus coming towards them, walking on the water, but fear took Peter by the throat.

"But Jesus immediately said to them: 'Take courage! It is I. Don't be afraid.' 'Lord, if it is you,' Peter replied, 'tell me to come to you on the water.' 'Come,' he said.

Then Peter got down out of the boat, walked on the water, and came toward Jesus. But when he saw the wind, he was afraid and, beginning to sink, cried out, 'Lord, save me!' Immediately, Jesus reached out his hand and caught him. 'You of little faith,' he said, 'why did you doubt?' And they climbed into the boat, the wind died down."

Matthew 14: 27-32 NIV

When I see Jesus in the middle of my storms, this scripture reminds me not to look down at the waves that seem to overtake me. Jesus is in the storms with us; our boats will rock and roll, but He promises to get us through and calm the seas.

Preparing Your Boat for Storms Ahead

I am no longer one half of a couple. Today, my boat is filled with lovely new friends. We've come to depend on each other for company and adventures and to fill space with laughter and friendship. These precious ones are in my life now because I made room for them to sit beside me. We help each other navigate the waters of life with grace and faith.

More storms of life are waiting up ahead, with angry winds to blow us off course. This is true, especially in times of grieving. A sunny day can turn dark quickly, and we can prepare by knowing who is alongside us and willing to set sail for new adventures. Fellow travelers make future storms less intimidating.

TRY THIS: WHO'S IN MY BOAT?

Your "boat" is likely very different from mine. Try to imagine your "boat" now. If it helps, consider the following questions and use them as journal prompts.

- What type of vessel are you maneuvering?
- Are you the lone captain calling all the shots? Or are there too many captains for one boat?
- Do you choose destinations only you can see?
- How are you navigating the water?
- What is the weather like as you've set sail?
- What kind of water is around you?

Draw your boat and the surrounding water on a separate piece of paper or your journal. There is no need for talent or skill; a simple doodle is fine for this activity.

Now, think of the other people in the boat on this journey with you. List or draw them, and describe what they mean to you in one word beside each name.

- Give yourself permission to express your true feelings, even if they might be "negative."
- Optional: Shred this to preserve ultimate privacy.

Your goal today is to list the people on your journey, no matter who they are. Describe them, then keep each name in your mind and pray for them. We are asked to pray for those we love and even our enemies. Over the next few weeks, notice what comes from praying for those in your metaphorical boat.

THE PEOPLE ON MY JOURNEY ARE...

THIRTY-TWO
RELAXING INTO YOUR WORRIES

> *"We don't have tomorrow yet. All we have is this moment. And...what are you going to do with it?"*
>
> Jeff Moore

WHETHER LIFE SEEMS full or not to you right now, whatever grief took from your life has left a hole, an empty place. It may not be obvious to others. Some of us have mastered covering it like frosting a cardboard cake. Or, your loss may have rearranged your entire life, visible to any observer. The part of you that's been taken is gone and can't be reattached in the same way, no matter how hard you try.

Widows can fall in love again and remarry, but the new husband will be his own person. A second marriage will always be different from the widow's first. Should I ever marry again, I would need to see a new husband with fresh eyes, accepting him as unique and not a remake of my late husband.

After the passing of a child, the blessing of pregnancy can happen. A new baby will not be a replacement but be a welcome addition to the family.

Newness can grow out of the ashes of loss when we are willing to nourish and accept a different way of living. A seed must be put into the soil for it to grow. That's where necessary nutrients and conditions are found. We can establish places in life for new people, places, opportunities, or circumstances to flourish. Faith is where our trust in God grows, and this is what plows the ground for a new thing.

One of the most quoted promises in scripture is this:

"And we know that in all things God works for the good of those who love Him, who have been called according to His purposes."

Romans 8:28 NIV

A common misconception of this verse is that all things that happen are "good"; instead, Paul is saying that all things can be transformed for our inner good, even hard things.

There are lessons I've learned that have only come from the crucible of pain and sorrow. These afflictions touched my soul and gave me a more profound understanding of balancing life, especially when it doesn't work out as I thought it should.

God sees the big picture of our lives all at the same time. He can work all things out, even obviously bad things. He works these things out by using them to draw us closer to Him.

I've permitted myself to do old things in a new way, and that's also helped allow space to reframe the things taken due to experiencing loss. For example, thanks to my seasoned widowhood, I now know how to venture out and feel more comfortable going to social gatherings, movies, out to dinner, and even church alone. In the past, doing these alone would've been daunting, unnecessary, or avoided altogether. As with anything else in life, practice makes it easier.

Trusting God when we have been emotionally or physically shaken gives an inner peace that waters the courage to step into new places. I can have confidence in someone greater than myself, someone who loves me completely. I can rest in the fact that,

> *"I can do all things through Christ who strengthens me."*
>
> Philippians 4:13 NKJV

Even alone, in my pain, while I'm healing, or with difficult people, I can do anything that's required of me, with Christ's strength holding me up. The Word also reminds us of the following.

> *"Blessed is the man who trusts in the LORD, whose trust is the LORD. He is like a tree planted by water, that sends out its roots by the stream, and does not fear when heat comes, for its leaves remain green, and is not anxious in the year of drought, for it does not cease to bear fruit."*
>
> Jeremiah 17:7-8 ESV

Trusting in the Lord means you can trust God for what you need. This is foundational to our Christian walk. Taking this trust one step deeper, we acknowledge trusting the Lord of all creation. He is worthy of our trust. He never fails us.

Trusting and relying on humans will ultimately fail. People disappoint, even unintentionally. For whatever reason, we hurt each other, even the ones we love.

Trusting God never fails. His trustworthiness is solid and complete. We can trust Him, no matter what drought springs up in our life. He can make all things alive, green, and flourishing.

> *"Trust in the Lord with all your heart and lean not on your own understanding; In all your ways acknowledge Him and He will make your path straight."*
>
> Proverbs 3:5 NIV

I've learned that my reliance on God grows with each step of trust I take toward Him. In return, I am filled with a willingness to trust Him more.

From freshly tilled soil, new life can come from our loss, which may be the catalyst to discover a fresh start. These fresh starts build upon the strength, courage, and purpose He teaches.

TRY THIS: RELAX INTO YOUR WORRIES

The *Oxford Language Dictionary* defines *trust* as a "firm belief in the reliability, truth, ability, or strength of someone or something."

The opposite of trust is *worry*. When going through times of suffering, there is plenty to worry about. It's easy to get caught in cycles of regret, doubts, or fears that come from worry, making the ground we're standing on feel even more unsure or scary.

Worry is permitting the mind to dwell on possibilities that have not happened or will not happen. Potential problems or situations are something we see or imagine to happen in the future.

Today, we will list those worries, whether small or overwhelming.

By making a list of the things you are worried about right now, these things can more easily be shifted into a place of trust, letting go of what is not a reality now. God wants to be the reliable strength of truth in your circumstances.

Use the space below to write out the things pressing into you and bringing worry. Be as specific as possible.

TODAY I'M WORRIED ABOUT:
1.
2.
3.
4.
5.

Once these worries are listed, use each one as a prayer starter and ask God to show you how to manage the specific thing that gives you worry right now. Ask Him to show you how to manage the stresses and fears that are heavy for you. Ask for peace about the issues, even if you see no way of resolve. All our Heavenly Father requires is to trust Him with what worries us most.

Today, treat yourself to a moment, an hour, or a relaxing day. Whatever form that takes for you:

- Reading.
- A bubble bath.
- A glass of wine on the porch.
- Eating with friends.
- Watching a sunset.
- A drive in the country.

Celebrate you and be blessed for the fullness that has grown. No matter how small or life-changing your newness is, be encouraged by the fruit growing from it.

I SPENT MY NEW DAY IN THE FOLLOWING WAYS...

THIRTY-THREE
SUFFERING & ENDURING

"Do not be anxious about anything, but in everything, by prayer and petition, with thanksgiving, present your request to God. And the peace of God, which transcends all understanding, will guard your hearts and your minds in Christ Jesus."

Philippians 4:6-7 NIV

AT ONE POINT OR ANOTHER, you may have caught yourself asking, "Why?" To mortal minds, it seems impossible for God to know everything and still allow such suffering in the world, including the sorrow that touches our lives personally.

Logic would follow that if God knew, He could stop, heal, and protect us from the harm of others—and yet, He doesn't always do it. This seems cruel, at least it does to me. Should we conclude from this that we are the victims of God's apathy?

No matter how strong your faith is, it's very human to want to shake a fist at God and be angry or at least feel hopeless; He didn't stop or change the circumstances of your suffering. I remember praying constantly for Him to heal the cancer that was destroying the body of my husband; I had faith that God could perform a solid miracle for him, and what a testimony of God's love and power that would be! I kept telling God my idea. But it didn't work out that way. Cancer was the winner.

It can be very discouraging and confusing not to have the answers or results we ask God for. These unanswered questions' spiritual and internal war on our soul can seep into every aspect of life. Anger, resentment, addiction, or even despair can quickly become the glasses used to view life as it is now. Those emotions can become debilitating and cloud how God wants to use suffering for a bigger purpose.

It's a faith choice. It's an attitude and a choice that says, "I don't understand. I'm hurting here, but I won't be crushed because I choose to hold on to God, who will make a way when I see no way."

> "The loss of a loved one, debilitating physical illness, a crippling accident, the adulterous betrayal of a spouse, sudden financial loss, the disloyalty of a friend or loved one, or the rebellion of a child are all very difficult experiences, but they do not define you, and they must not be taken on as your identity."
>
> Paul David Tripp, *Suffering* (p. 131)

We have an identity in Christ as His children, and we are His sons and daughters. Suffering transforms us; we are never the same, having survived the hardest trials. Let God use these days to teach you who He is and how much He loves you *through* your grief.

Bad things do happen. Cars crash, cancer grows, husbands leave, people betray us—the list goes on and on.

So, how do we reconcile a loving God who sometimes seems to sit back and allow pain and anguish to happen?

We don't. We can't understand it, and we can't fully reconcile it.

Yes, God knows. He allows. He sees it all.

Furthermore, He understands your grief.

For hopefully obvious reasons, those are easy words to read or write. Perhaps it is easier to do when life is going smoothly. However, when life punches us in the stomach, these answers can be fighting words.

A well-meaning friend or neighbor with good intentions attempting to offer a crumb of comfort can unintentionally trigger our anger, resentment, overwhelm, and unintentionally hurt us.

During early grief processing, I've experienced many days wishing someone would say absolutely nothing and just sit beside me. Silence is less painful when it is not filled with phrases like "You can always have more children," "This was God's will," or "It was for the best."

ACCEPTING TRUTHS

At some point during the grieving process, there will come a time for accepting the truths held within the following three scriptures.

Psalm 91 is one of my favorite passages in scripture. I encourage you to read the entire chapter, especially when feeling lost in your grief. It's always been a comfort.

> *"He who dwells in the shelter of the Most High will rest in the shadow of the Almighty. I will say of the Lord, "He is my refuge and my fortress, my God, in whom I trust."*
>
> Psalm 91: 1-2 NIV

God sees our suffering and will use it if we allow Him to take it for our healing.

> *"And the God of all grace, who called you to His eternal glory in Christ, after you have suffered a little while, will himself restore you and make you strong, firm and steadfast."*
>
> 1 Peter 5:10 NIV

If today is not the day for this kind of coming to terms, file this scripture away for whenever the time is right.

> *"The Lord is close to the brokenhearted and saves those who are crushed in spirit."*
>
> Psalm 34:18 NIV

Your version of "coming to terms with things" will look or sound different from how it happened or feels for me today. I can't tell you exactly how that process will look, but I can tell you that it's been a slow, gradual, steady sense of knowing and inner peace. I have confidence that God will heal you in the way that you need to be healed, as he did with me.

God knows how to chop up the pieces of grief into manageable pieces to allow digestion. Smaller bites of huge helpings are the only way to get through this kind of pain, hour-by-hour, moment-by-moment.

This doesn't change the fact that grief isn't sleek or comfy. Grief is still bumpy and rocky, and it hurts.

One way that my healing arrived was through the smaller, bite-sized acknowledgment and acceptance that He, too, knows the sorrow of anguish and heartache.

The shortest verse in the Bible is about grief.

"Jesus wept."

John 11:35 NIV

Talk about bite-sized truth!

The grieving sisters of Lazarus, a good friend of Jesus, just confronted him with the news of their brother's death. Reading further into the account, Jesus knew a miracle would soon be demonstrated, raising Lazarus back to life. Yet, His compassion and deep human emotion gave way to tears of sorrow. Jesus sympathizes with our pain. Scripture tells us,

---

"For we do not have a high priest who is unable to sympathize with our weaknesses..."

Hebrews 4:15 NIV

Okay, so Jesus can sympathize with us, but what good is that when our world still crashes and burns around our feet?

The concept that God controls all things is called the Sovereignty of God. It means that He is leading all things, no matter what.

"For by Him all things were created: things in heaven and on earth, visible and invisible, whether thrones or powers or rulers or authorities; all things were created by Him and for Him. He is before all things, and in Him, all things hold together."

Colossians 1:16-17 NIV

In general, we are faced with the choice of who we trust. Do we trust only ourselves and our own sovereignty? Do we trust God and God's sovereignty?

No matter what we find ourselves in the middle of (even our own sovereignty), there is a Savior who loves us and who we can trust, whose knowledge surpasses our limited understanding. It's understandable to be uncomfortable or unwilling to trust someone we don't know. This is where surrender and choosing to build a relationship can bring peace that passes understanding.

TRY THIS: GOD IS BIGGER THAN TIME

I read the quote on the following page from Roy Lessin when my days get out of control. It carries a simple truth to it in a big way. God knows.

As you read through it, note any sentence or section that speaks to you or particularly impacts your thinking. Jot down the small section and carry it on a sticky note or a small scrap of paper.

"God is bigger than time,
dates, and appointments.
He wants you to move
through this day with a quiet heart,
an inward assurance that
He is in control, a peaceful certainty
that your life is in His hands,
a deep trust in His plan and purposes,
and a thankful disposition,
toward all that He allows.
He wants you to put your faith in Him,
not in a timetable.
He wants you to wait on Him and wait for Him.
In His perfect way, He will put everything
together, see to every detail...
arrange every circumstance...
and order every step to bring
to pass what He has for you."

Roy Lessin[*]

---

[*] This poem is also available at this link: https://www.azquotes.com/author/64016-Roy_Lessin

THIRTY-FOUR
ONE BALLOON AT A TIME

> *"Therefore, if anyone is in Christ, he is a new creation; the old has gone, the new has come!"*
>
> 2 Corinthians 5:17 NIV

A FRESH START can happen anytime along your journey. Major life events of any size allow one to take a new look at life. For many of us, these events become turning points.

Our insides try to cushion the blows from loss and grief. We feel the swelling and painful bruises, looking for escape. I encourage taking great care during these moments.

Depression, loneliness, isolation, even anger, and defeat can feel like easier pills to swallow than the task of leaving your comfort zone. Swallowing these pills of anger and defeat can give false hopes and cloud the eyes. I've learned this the hard way. Leaning upon depressive feelings and nursing our wounds with isolation and its emotional cousins are usually dull weapons for getting through our pain. For me, they never work well and never work for long.

Externally speaking, your surroundings may have changed and don't look the same. Often, seasons of grief prompt a change of scenery that can feel unfamiliar or improper.

> *"I waited patiently for the Lord; he turned to me and heard my cry. He lifted me out of the slimy pit and out of the mud and mire; He set my feet on a rock and gave me a firm place to stand. He put a new song in my mouth, a hymn of praise to our God. Many will see and fear and put their trust in the Lord."*
>
> Psalm 40:1-3 NIV

Since you're in a new environment, let's try using some new tools to find a renewed sense of comfort, meaning, and home in your surroundings.

One such tool is simply moving forward, one step at a time, to pick up the broken pieces of life. Daily life can be made new again, maybe not the same as before, but familiar in a fresh way. Some days, this tool might be as small as getting out of bed.

On other days, it will feel like standing in a room with helium balloons filling the ceiling--a ballroom filled with an overwhelming forest of long ribbons at eye level. Each balloon needs our attention and represents a project, responsibility, pressing issue, and big or small decision.

After the dust settled when my husband died, I was faced with the task of putting my life back together without him. In those early days, I imagined my ceiling filled with helium balloons, each with an attached chore for me to deal with. In my mind, I would lower a balloon, work on the issue as much as possible, and then let the unfinished balloon float back to join all the other things that needed to be tended to. One "balloon" at a time, I worked my way through tying up his life and shifting mine around.

In the early days of my grief, I knew that everything pushing against the ceiling needed to be dealt with, and I also knew I was capable of pulling one string to hold one balloon at a time. It felt like I could never finish any task or project, prompting the balloon to float back up to the ceiling to wait for its next turn.

He makes us new. "Therefore, if anyone is in Christ, he is a new creation; the old has gone, the new has come!"

2 Corinthians 5:17 NIV

Transformation takes a faith mindset that your life is big enough to embrace brand-new pieces, places, and things and that God is trustworthy enough to show you. He can reveal your heart. We can't heal ourselves. Time makes hurt smaller in the distance, but time by itself doesn't completely heal either.

Yet, miraculous power can be found in the name of Jesus.

"Therefore God exalted Him to the highest place and gave Him the name that is above every name, that at the name of Jesus every knee should bow, in heaven and on earth and under the earth, and every tongue confess that Jesus Christ is Lord to the glory of God the Father."

Philippians 2:9-11. NIV

Asking Him to save you and forgive the sin that weighs you down, He will make all things new, even you. He will regenerate your soul and heal your heart.

"In reply, Jesus declared, 'I tell you the truth, no one can see the kingdom of God unless he is born again.' 'How can a man be born when he is old?' Nicodemus asked. 'Surely he cannot enter a second time into his mother's womb to be born!' Jesus answered, 'I tell you the truth, no one can enter

> *the kingdom of God unless he is born of water and the Spirit. Flesh gives birth to flesh, but the Spirit gives birth to the spirit."*
>
> John 3: 3-6 NIV

God can take the destructive emotions from us, and we need Christ to give us peace of mind and a new life.

> *"Peace I leave with you; my peace I give you. I do not give peace to you as the world gives. Do not let your hearts be troubled, and do not be afraid."*
>
> John 14:27 NIV

Be honest with yourself today. If you've never asked Jesus to take over your life, you can. He will give you the joy and peace of God, which the world can never give you.

A new life in Christ makes for a new you.

> *The power of Jesus can fill your life, the power that gives joy when nothing is going right. "For it is by grace you have been saved, through faith— and this not from yourselves, it is the gift of God— not by works, so that no one can boast."*
>
> Ephesians 2:8 NIV

TRY THIS: FIND NEW MEANING IN MUSIC

Pick some music that you know is guaranteed to lift your spirit. Personally, I like to listen to praise and worship music. I hook my phone up to a Bluetooth speaker and let my whole house fill with music that uplifts my soul.

You might be a praise music champ or love classical, jazz, or your favorite dance teacher's music playlist. Regardless of the music genre, this exercise should boost your audio environment to explore how sound and music affect your overall mood throughout the day.

An extra challenge: if you've never listened to praise or worship music, find some and see how your soul is blessed by it.

THIRTY-FIVE
COMFORT IN CLARITY (RECIPE: COMFORT CREAMY POTATO SOUP)

"People, even more than things, have to be restored, renewed, revived, reclaimed, and redeemed: never throw out anyone."

Audrey Hepburn

MY PRAYER IS that the readings so far have been a help to you during this time of grief. Not all help feels warm and fuzzy. Sometimes, it's the strong arms that pack up the moving boxes. Other times, it's the flick of a pen that writes the note you really need.

But there are days during grief when the kind of help we *really* want is comfort, not necessarily the practical kind. These are the days we want an old pair of sweatpants and a familiar movie. Maybe for you those days sound like someone calling you up to surprise you with dinner plans (instead of you doing all the legwork yourself). Maybe your comfort days sound like canceling all the plans so you can lay on the couch and do nothing.

No matter your comfort needs, I've found that when our comfort is most needed, this is also the easiest time to get lost in the desert and weeds of grief.

Finding Comfort in Friendships

Accepting the new reality after your loss takes time and is uncomfortable, but it can be done. With practice, your reality will also find a new comfort.

Loss, no matter what kind, is personal and important to us. Whatever hole that's opened up can eventually be filled with new friends, new living arrangements, a new pet, or even a new purpose. I've come to realize how comfortable friends can make life, especially now that my spouse is gone. In my husband, I took my friends for granted because I had a listening ear, support, and assistance whenever I needed it in a husband. Now, those things are not taken for granted and therefore valued more. Friends have always been there for me, but now they are essential.

Finding Comfort in Clarity

Insight comes from being in the middle of a circumstance while looking for answers. Especially when everything in life feels messy and complicated, this is when we're craving comfort from clarity. I encourage you to take these times to stay open to seeing things differently. God will give you fresh eyes to see new things in your life. These are new chapters waiting to be written.

Be ready for God to fill you with a new purpose. Keep your eyes and ears open. You can inspire other people, so make sure to tell your story. Others need to hear it.

As we grow more comfortable with the new way things are now, it becomes easier to come alongside other people who are also facing hard times. We need each other. We can have compassion for others who are hurting because we know hurt and heartbreak ourselves.

Finding Comfort in Community

Don't float for too long in the boat of isolation. It might feel restful to be away from a life in upheaval for a time, at least from the noise and chaos it brings. But we are designed to be in a community and share life with others.

Not only do we need others, but other people need us. They need the compassion we're acquiring today during this season of grief. You and I know what heartbreak feels like. You and I will see pain in someone else's eyes because we've known it, too.

TRY THIS: A RECIPE - COMFORT CREAMY POTATO SOUP

For today's recipe, I'm sharing my favorite go-to for when I need something warm and filling: **Comfort Creamy Potato Soup**. I've found it's always good to have an easy soup on hand that can be ready quickly, especially when comfort food is needed for yourself or to share. This is a good recipe for dropping off a large jar to anyone who needs a little food-hug. Add some frozen yeast rolls and a warm meal to comfort your tummy.

Comfort Creamy Potato Soup

Ingredients

- 3–5 pounds of potatoes
- 1–2 cartons of chicken stock or vegetable broth
- Toppings (optional): Shredded cheese, Bacon, Onion straws, Fresh chopped chives

Directions

1. 3–5 pounds of potatoes. Peel and cut into quarters potatoes and place in your soup pot.
2. 1–2 cartons of chicken stock or vegetable broth. Add broth or stock to cover the potatoes.
3. Bring to a boil until the potatoes are tender and cooked.
4. Don't drain the cooking liquid.
5. Use an immersion blender or potato masher to mash the cooked potatoes in the stock liquid. You can smooth the

potatoes as much as you like or leave some potato pieces for a chunkier soup.
6. While the potatoes are still hot, add half to a whole block of softened cream cheese.
7. Allow the cream cheese to melt into the soup, using the immersion blender or potato masher to ensure it's incorporated.
8. The texture or thickness of the soup is up to you. If you like a thinner version, add a little half-and-half or milk to get it to your liking. (I like it thick) Sometimes, I add some corn here to add a sweet crunch to the soup—salt and pepper to taste.

TA-DA! A comfort potato soup that's filling, good, and effortless!

Share some **Comfort Creamy Potato Soup** with someone who needs a loving example of God's love in you.

WEEK SIX: FINDING MEANING IN REMEMBERING

"What we have once enjoyed and deeply loved we can never lose, for all that we love deeply becomes a part of us."

Helen Keller

THIRTY-SIX
CELEBRATING WITHIN GRIEF

"Celebration comes when the common features of life are redeemed."

Richard J. Foster

TODAY MARKS an important day of celebration, the first day of our final week in this book. Depending on your current circumstances, a celebration might be the farthest thing from your heart right now, especially if life is still filled with heavy pain. If that is you, I encourage you to stick with me today.

Celebration is a powerful tool, regardless of your current mood. It's a word that marks a special day or event. The word "celebrate" in Hebrew is translated *as hagag,* which means "to prepare, keep or observe." Of course, we've experienced firsthand how grief has a place in the realm of *hagag*. Through witnessing the many fellow sojourners in grief, I've seen even more ways that our hurts can be softened by celebrating, remembering, or keeping treasured what is lost.

Is Grief a Contronym?

In many ways, people hear the word "grief" and think sad, gloomy thoughts. They usually do not think of the additional meaning it can hold: celebration. Grief can become a contronym, especially for those who understand the depth and power of the change that grief can bring to a person's life.

Contronyms are words that have multiple definitions with opposite meanings. For instance, "dust" can be dusted *off* furniture and sugar-dusted *onto* baked goods. We can also clip papers *together* or clip *off* some long fingernails. Just as one coin has two sides, one word can have opposite meanings.

I've found this is true for grief, too. We can be sad *and* celebrate simultaneously.

This is not to be confused with failed attempts to put on a happy face. We still have permission to be Debbie Downer with this kind of grief celebration. Our celebration within grief (not the celebration of grief) doesn't diminish or subtract from the sadness or the pain experienced. On the other side of sorrow, still, *within* the bounds of grieving, there is a possibility for genuine celebration, the kind of celebration that would not require a mask to cover tearful moments that may arise.

The Object of Celebration is NOT Equal to the Source of Grief

To be clear, the source of a person's grief is not always the object of the celebration found within that grief.

For example, the source of my grief was the loss of family members, but celebration was found during grief through remembering. However, another person might celebrate the discovery of liberation and internal strength that came from a difficult and painful divorce.

It's understandable the desire to avoid the celebration of pain, especially pain experienced from harm, victimization, health loss, betrayal, or worse. That is not what I'm asking you to consider today.

Instead of celebrating the event or source that caused or created your pain, I challenge you to celebrate the many ways you've changed and grown as a result of or *despite* your pain.

Although suffering can be a powerful teacher, without moments to stop, breathe, and celebrate, even the strongest among us can crash and burn out.

Celebration allows us the opportunity to learn things about ourselves that we wouldn't have learned otherwise. It's at least worth small moments to celebrate this growth.

Celebrating allows the opportunity to observe the progress you've made on your private grief journey. It allows you to choose your mindset towards the difficulties you're facing. We can't change circumstances, but we can allow God to use them to shape us into stronger, more compassionate people.

"Be joyful always; pray continually; give thanks in all circumstances, for this is God's will for you in Christ Jesus."

1 Thessalonians 5:16 NIV

I've emphasized "in" above because Paul advises the Thessalonian Christians to be joyful, pray, and give thanks in(side) of all circumstances. God's will is for us to experience joy and pray throughout the hard days rather than obstruct joy until things turn around.

While there is a fine line at times, there is still a difference between giving thanks *for* the painful circumstance (looking back in time) and giving thanks with*in* the circumstance (while it's still happening). Paul isn't asking us to celebrate painful occurrences but instead asking that we allow God to use the circumstances to help others going through similar hurts.

Paul instructs us on the three things to do while suffering: be joyful always, pray continually, and give thanks. Part of our decision is to choose our behaviors and be thankful or celebrate even when we don't feel like it, when life is far from a good time, or when there's nothing to celebrate. It's easy to feel a victim of the circumstance you find yourself in: poor health, a horrible marriage, abandonment through death or loss, disillusionment; you name it—it's bad—nothing to be happy about.

During times when isolation feels comfortable but can be equally unhealthy, look for opportunities to celebrate with others. These opportunities can become a welcome excuse to ignore the grips of isolation. While the enemy uses isolation to point us toward dark holes that are challenging to climb out of, prioritizing celebration and joy turns on a light in our soul to shine on the darker days.

The spiritual practice of celebrating life with others isn't a party for one.

Celebrating life with others is a way to share your story with those who need to hear it. We have no idea how those in our sphere of influence watch how we react to what life has thrown our way.

After my husband died, I returned to work at the Yarn Shop I owned. I was surprised to hear from a few employees that some newer customers had labeled me the "sad lady." I thought I was putting on an all-is-well, happy-face mask. Apparently, my pain was seeping out in social exchanges through ways I couldn't control.

As the years progressed and I became more secure in my grief journey, I was often told how strong and peaceful I appeared after tromping through my losses. We may not be aware of it now, but other people observe clues and witness how we keep going when life tries to stop us.

For me, these moments with observers are perfect opportunities to share who I am and how much my faith in God provides courage and inner joy to keep going and growing.

Hurt is a common and universal experience. We get to remember this commonality and support each other when we celebrate. Additionally, these celebrations become a strengthening factor in your relationship with the Lord.

As I mentioned earlier in Week 1, after my son died, our family was dreading the first anniversary of his passing. We decided to celebrate by renaming the date "Mark's Heaven birthday." The name gave a new spin on a day that loomed full of sadness. The tradition of choosing to celebrate heaven made all the difference. It's a practice my daughter and I continued again when George died, and we mark those anniversaries of heaven still today. It continues to remind us to be joyful.

TRY THIS: JOURNAL PROMPT

No matter the depth of your painful circumstances now, ask God today to show you how to choose celebration, even if it's for one day or in the smallest way.

My prayer for you is that every day you celebrate will build your strength.

Write for as long as your heart needs to tell you something. Set a timer if that's helpful. Remember, this celebration concept isn't a "yippee! Let's party! I'm in pain!" session. It's a mindset change to ask how God can and will show you new things.

HOLDING SADNESS IN ONE HAND AND CELEBRATION IN THE OTHER FEELS LIKE...

THIRTY-SEVEN
REMINISCE

"Life can only be understood backwards, but it must be lived forwards."

Søren Kierkegaard

Yesterday, we discussed new meanings to celebration within our grieving process. This would naturally get one's headspace primed for reminiscing.

Reminisce helps connect a person to their past, an important step in accepting how life unfolds. Sharing and remembering personal experiences and stories about meaningful relationships provides an opportunity to reflect upon life as it was and how it is now.

In aging, there is documented evidence that reminiscence can play a role in the process of helping people come to terms with their lives. Reminiscing can help people define who they are now and who they used to be. Sharing memories brings people together, laughter, and feelings of being connected. It also provides an opportunity to come to terms with the things that didn't get accomplished or dreams that didn't turn out as expected.

Grief has the same issues to face. Shared memories can bring community and a sense of joyful memory. At the same time, reminiscing about a loss or time of suffering can cause us to look at circumstances that feel raw and painful. Loss has buried inside it hopes and dreams that go unfilled. That becomes the part of grieving that is so difficult to reconnect with. It's not fair that a young mom dies and leaves her children, or a husband takes up with a new family and turns his back on the one he has, or that driver crosses the yellow line, and the accident gives a life of pain and limitation. The list goes on and on of unfair, rotten life deals.

We, as mourners, have the opportunity to keep moving ahead in the life we have now and reminiscing can play a part.

It's important to come to terms with our loves, losses, experiences, accomplishments, and failures. The act of reminiscing is built into each of us.

I realized the importance of reminiscing in a most roundabout way. Returning to college after dropping out of nursing school my last quarter, I was eager to start a new study plan. That's when I bumped into a most unlikely friend who changed the course of my life. She was a free-spirit poet who happened to teach a poetry writing class in a nursing home. She was planning a tea party and felt out of her comfort zone. Party planning and entertaining have always been my love, so I agreed to help her organize the party. I knew nothing about poetry or nursing homes but loved a good tea party.

When I entered the activity room where the class was held, I was amazed by the joy these older folks exhibited. Trapped in bodies that no longer worked as they once did, life was reduced to a twin bed and a favorite chair; they were full. They were full of excitement to have two young people come to share the outside world with them, but mostly, they loved telling their stories and being listened to.

That was the start of another Major change in college study that eventually led to a master's degree in gerontology, the study of aging. I took over the running of the poetry group when my friend left the country to live on a kibbutz in Israel.

I realized the poetry I brought to the class every week was bigger than reading lovely words together. It sparked life from their memories of the past and lively discussion of who they were and their life's journey.

We wrote our poetry from the memories each member shared.

Each week, I brought a piece of poetry to read, and then the residents and I would write a collaborative poem. I gave my students the first line, and they finished the sentence. Collected sentences were read aloud, each one a line of our group poem.

For example, one prompt was "The quietest thing I remember..." This provided an opportunity to reminisce about a quiet memory. This phrase alone was enough to launch my students into a moment from long ago. Here's an example of what that prompt produced:

Quiet
The quietest thing...
I walked into a pine forest and stepped on needles
the quietest, softest feeling I lever heard.
The beauty of the quiet sunset on the mountains gently falling
  asleep.
The lone tick-tock of the clock in an empty room full of people.
The quietest thing...
The happiness I can feel when I think of someone I love.
Love is a quiet feeling.
The sun as it goes down in the west in its gowns of color.
Opening the door early to get the morning paper and seeing
  snow everywhere, sensing the quiet and beauty of it.

Hawthorne Nursing Home, Vintage Poetry Group (Vintage Verse for Lisa, 1979)

The day we wrote that collaborative poem, the eyes of each participant told me the words they shared were attached to much deeper memories. Memory transplants us to other places and times. The students in this poetry class were all in their 80s or 90s. For some, I was the scribe of their thoughts, as the physical task of writing was no longer possible. Be assured that each line was written independently, gathered around reminiscing about the topic, *quiet*. The thoughts were collected into a poem by reminiscing. Words gave a voice to their memories.

Reminiscing with others gives life to the past. It can bring happiness, or it can bring regrets. It can shed light on things that are too late to do or accomplish. In either case, there is a place for coming to terms with our past to live in peace in our present.

The beauty of reminiscing can be found in the opportunity it provides for coming to terms with any regrets that may arise. It's not only a job of old age, but there is purpose in looking back and remembering at any age. Giving a voice to a memory is an important part of healing and accepting the past. Also, it's for others who need to hear as much as it is for the person who needs to verbalize it.

Reminiscing is the way to recall what you had, who was in your life, what you enjoyed, or what's missing. It's an important way of settling choices, events, relationships, and more. Reminiscing gives memories a place to exist, become ordered, and smoothed out. It's as if our brain can now fold these moments, which were once confusing or fading, and tuck each memory away to pull out if/when needed in the future.

One of the most precious gifts God has given us is our memories. And one of the most important things we can do is remember His faithfulness in the past. That gives us the hope to trust Him today, stepping on the solid pavement He has already laid down.

He saved you and walked you through past hurts and hard days. Remembering those moments about your relationship with Him is a wonderful testimony to share with others while inviting Him to do it again. And again.

TRY THIS: FINDING MEANING IN REMEMBERING

"I thank my God every time I remember you."

Philippians 1:3 NIV

When you read that scripture above, who do you think of? Who else? Take today to fill your mind and heart and pray for someone who touched your life in the past. Remember how they shaped you, helped you, or held you.

Sit quietly for a few minutes and think of that person(s). Put those thoughts into a sentence or a singular word that describes them. Journal or say a prayer for the person who came to mind.

Even if that person is gone or not in your life today, it's comforting to remember that God gives us blooms of joy through the people on our path. Make a note below to remember who you prayed for, especially today.

Today, I'm remembering the following person:

- How did this person touch your life in good ways?
- Which memories bring up the fondest feelings about this person? List as many as you'd like.
- What lessons did they or their presence teach you?
- How do you know your life is different today because of their influence?
- How might you share what you learned from them with someone else?

THIRTY-EIGHT
MEMORY LANE

"Nostalgia: A device that removes the ruts and potholes from memory lane."

Doug Larson

THERE'S a fine line between our memories, nostalgia and reminiscing. **Memories** are the brain's interpretation of past events. Looking back on memories can bring feelings of happiness but also shots of sadness.

Memories also hold a key that can unlock a feeling of well-being, joy, strength, levity, and success. Thinking back at how you influenced a big project at work or bent down and captured a teachable moment with your child, these are reasons to remember. We can touch the lives of those around us in ways we may not realize.

Reminiscing might look like talking or thinking about those memories, good or bad. However, I consider **nostalgia** more of a longing for or wishing for times past.

Grief or sadness can nestle in the recesses of nostalgia. Many times, these feelings are hidden like an underground geyser. The pressure of memory and loss can build up to the point of explosion, leaving you crying in the middle of the grocery store. Don't let the fear of expressing certain emotions prevent you from experiencing the joy of nostalgia.

Don't get me wrong. Nostalgia is not always about the good times. There can be regret or pain in nostalgia. There's a sort of comfort in nostalgia, especially when we're in *unfamiliar* seasons of newness. Nostalgia can feel comfortable yet painful when we look back on *familiar* times of hurt, pain, apologies, abuse, disappointment—the list goes on.

Perhaps this kind of nostalgia is one of the many reasons why it is so easy to find oneself returning to toxic or abusive relationship cycles. It feels comfy compared to our current unfamiliar and new possibilities to the old ones.

However, this comparison of time (past vs. now) can bolster our memories. Our memories honor accomplishments throughout the grieving process. Not forgetting past moments can be a barometer to gauge how life is now.

Nostalgia can boost feelings of happiness or time well spent. For instance, remembering a vacation at the beach, a great hike in the mountains, or a family reunion—these feelings can be re-lived when we remember those moments. The way life was then may not be what life is now, and that's okay because we can still access those moments through our memories.

Nostalgia is also about sharing memories with others and can bring people closer. A picture is worth a thousand words. I can view snapshots of places I've never been with people I don't know and still appreciate the sentimental impact. Finding old photographs of long-gone relatives can bring feelings of nostalgia for a time when we weren't even born yet.

Using nostalgia or looking back on when times were "better" or at least different can have a place in the grieving journey. A trip down memory lane, especially when in grief, can be used as a coping tool to help transition through seasons of loneliness or sadness.

According to Dr. Krystine Batcho, PhD a professor at Le Moyne College, her research on the psychology of nostalgia explains,

> "The word was coined or invented a long time ago, over 300 years ago, and originally designated homesickness. Well, semantic drift over the centuries has broadened that to the notion of longing for or missing aspects of a person's personal lived past. That is the kind of nostalgia or that is what I mean when I talk about nostalgia and it's a wonderfully complex paradoxical experience."
>
> Dr. Krystine Batcho, PhD

In her interview Dr. Batcho later says:[*]

> "Most of the research available today, including my research, argues that nostalgia serves a number of functions. The thing that ties them all together is that nostalgia is an emotional experience that unifies. One example of this is it helps to unite our sense of who we are, our self, our identity over time. Because over time we change constantly, we change in incredible ways. We're not anywhere near the same as we were when we were three years old, for example. Nostalgia, by motivating us to remember the past in our own life, helps to unite us to that authentic self and remind us of who we have been and then compare that to who we feel we are today."
>
> Dr. Krystine Batcho, PhD on Episode 93 of Speaking of Psychology, American Psychological Association

---

[*] *https://www.apa.org/news/podcasts/speaking-of-psychology/nostalgia*

Dr. Batcho makes significant points about nostalgia, which certainly has benefits. However, as with any emotional concept, there is a dangerous side. We can't go back to the past. We can use it to soften or understand the present and bring us current joy and a sense of knowing, but it's not a place to reside.

"Do not say, 'Why were the old days better than these?' For it is not wise to ask such questions."

Ecclesiastes 7:10 NIV

Solomon, who wrote the wisdom book of Scripture called Ecclesiastes, warns of the dangers of holding too tightly onto the past. While there is a space for nostalgia and good reason not to forget the past, the Bible warns us not to live there. We can use our past to propel us into our future and be strengthened by remembering God's provisions in the past. That's a good reminder of His care, understanding, and lessons learned, no matter how hard. However, loneliness, pain, grief, and sorrow can trigger a longing for the past that isn't healthy. We miss the present and what the future has in store when shackled to the past.

"God spoke to Moses, "I've listened to the complaints of the Israelites. Now tell them: 'At dusk you will eat meat and at dawn you'll eat your fill of bread; and you'll realize that I am GOD, your God.'"

Exodus 16:11-12 MSG

The Israelites became grumblers, fearing Moses didn't know what he was doing, leading them on the journey through the wilderness. They began looking back at the life they had left, complaining how much better it was, even though they were slaves under brutal conditions. This time, nostalgia backfired, and God became angry at the ungrateful and angry attitudes it produced. God came through, however, and gave all the necessary provisions. Food was provided both day and night. God met them in their complaining and designed the solution.

Don't let nostalgia for yesterday cause you to miss God's gifts today. Memories and remembering certainly are important, but don't park there and forgo the lessons and growth from going through the fires of suffering. God is making you gold and will use your hard times.

Nostalgia is good, helpful, healthy, and can be part of the healing process while grieving. It can bring bittersweet emotions as memories are kindled with reminders of loss and good times. Use nostalgia wisely; it can serve you well along your grief journey.

There's purpose in the trials you walk through; don't miss the lesson. When you get to the other side of now, you will look back and be amazed at who you have become.

TRY THIS: MAKE A CONNECTION

Take some time today to look back and notice how memories make your physical body feel in the present. Then, take some time to write a note to someone or someplace in that memory. Consider your words on paper as a way of refreshing or sealing the moment.

Note: There is no pressure to look back on a *particular* season of your life. Simply select any past season that feels appropriate for your current season of grief and the purpose of today's exercise.

1. Look through some photos and allow your memories to connect with them. Even if you don't have personal photos nearby, glimpses of another person or place will likely hold a connection to a personal memory for you. If you have a photo album or pictures on your phone, get comfortable and go through some snapshots. The people, places, and memories captured there are part of you and always will be. Notice how they make you feel and let your mind expand the memory represented.

2. When you find a photo that captivates your memory in a particular way, make that image your anchor point for today.
3. If your memories hold people, take time to write them a note. If you feel inspired, reach out and text, call, or write a note that you are remembering them today. Contacting them might not be possible, but you can write a note anyway.
4. If your memories don't hold another person, I encourage you to write a letter to that location. For instance, if the photo or memory is of a scene from a specific location, you could start the letter with something like, "Dear Yellowstone National Park, Thank you for hosting that camping trip in 1991…"

You'll be surprised how words on paper enrich and heal our memories, even if there's no recipient.

Sending the letter is, of course, optional.

THIRTY-NINE
CELEBRATING MILESTONES

"The rain came down, the streams rose, and the winds blew and beat against that house; yet it did not fall, because it had its foundation on the rock."

Matthew 7:25 NIV

A MILESTONE MARKS a new chapter in life. A graduation, a new family member, or the death of a loved one, they mark us. These events, be they happy or crushing, are like a tree planted by water. Our life nourishes the event by the change that has been made. Milestones have a purpose; they mark transition and change. They denote something significant has taken place. A grief event can alter everything. It makes its own milestones.

In early grief, every day can seem like a milestone, just getting through it. I remember the crushing pain that woke me every morning. I carried it inside, feeling as if my chest would burst. This kind of suffering can be silent, unseen by others, as we learn how to maneuver through the tasks life requires. There's a lot of new learning when grief makes its way into a life. The hardest part is teaching yourself how to go on. That takes time and effort. Those who are left must pick up the pieces of what grief has shattered. I know because I've done it, and more than once.

Milestones are still in front of me all these years later. As my life progresses and years pass more quickly than I can watch, I've learned to accept family milestones alone. I wish I could have shared them with the people I've lost. My daughter's master's and doctoral degree ceremony, her wedding, and the birth of two beautiful babies are family milestones I marked alone, without my husband or parents to celebrate the joy. I know you have your altered milestones as well. Their importance isn't diminished or reduced; they are just made different because of the change that loss produces.

Milestones are all around us; anniversaries, birthdays, holidays, and vacations are all obvious. But if you think about it, life is full of moments that mark us.

Remembering experiences, plans, events, people, or situations shape us. We are bombarded with thousands of images daily, but not all hold space in our memory. What makes the difference is the emotion we attach to what we see and take in.

I've driven the route from my home in Kentucky to North Carolina hundreds of times, passing the same exits, landmarks, and fast food selections. The route doesn't change. When I'm listening to an interesting audiobook read over my Bluetooth device, I hardly remember the seven-hour drive. It seems as if I leave home, and the next thing I know, I've arrived.

But I remember a particular incident when driving back. I was the first in line when the officer shut down the Interstate. The cars in front of me were waved on to proceed; they shut down traffic in front of my car. I had a front-row viewing of the whole rescue scene.

Today, when I drive the same route, I can easily find the spot on the Interstate where the tree supported the jaws of life for first responders. Further still, I don't have to be at that tree to recall how I felt that day. I only need to remember that tree or see a tree that looks similar to me to feel the sympathetic wave of adrenaline wash over me.

You might have similar anchor points for your memories, too. Milestones, known as significant events, happen more often than we realize. Sure, a promotion, a birthday, or a new house are all common examples, but in quiet ways, we pass through milestones that mark us, especially in grief.

Of course, there is the grief event itself. This is the line in the sand that starts the journey.

From that day forward, things have changed.

Moving through the occurrence, the first year is a year of painful firsts. Every piece of life feels the loss. It's a hard year, perhaps the second or third year even harder, anticipating the pain that normal events highlight. Holidays, birthdays, vacations, solo couple's outings, family dinners, even Friday nights or Saturday errands alone bring reminders that life has changed. And it has. By that point, it's changed significantly.

No matter how many people are in your circle now, grief is a solo ride. Others can sit next to you, but the loss is your experience. And the loss is uniquely theirs as well. The journey rollercoaster is how we fit the round peg into a square hole to come to terms with the situation. Hold on.

Holding on is the key. What are you holding on to? The unchanging hand of God is the answer. All other things are sinking sand. The fog of life can be thick and blinding to the hand of God that is outstretched looking for yours.

"Therefore, everyone who hears these words of mine and puts them into practice is like a wise man who built his house on the rock. The rain came down, the streams rose, and the winds blew and beat against that house; yet it did not fall, because it had its foundation on the rock. But everyone

who hears these words of mine and does not put them into practice is like a foolish man who built his house on sand, the rain came down and the streams rose, and the winds blew and beat against that house, and it fell with a great crash."

Matthew 7:24-27 NIV

A milestone is a marker set up alongside the road to mark a particular place. God sees your spot on the road today. He is the rock we need now and always. Make sure you are standing on Him.

A milestone has the concept of achievement attached to it. Our kids hit developmental milestones in mastering skills like crawling, skipping, or reading. Noticing our son Mark wasn't hitting any milestones by nine months, we took him to be evaluated and realized what we suspected all along. At nine months, he hadn't mastered holding his head up by himself. All his motor skills were very lacking, and we knew something wasn't right deep down. He was put at a six-week developmental stage at nine months old. That knowledge set us down a narrow path of parenting a developmentally delayed child. Later, we learned he had a genetic deletion on his 15th chromosome, and, at the time, he was the 47th reported case of this particular disorder in the world.

Mark's milestones were unique to him in all ways, and the nine years we were privileged to have him with us on this earth proved that even the smallest thing can be celebrated. There is much joy in small things.

In your grief walk, don't forget that. A milestone doesn't necessarily need to be a huge accomplishment or wait for an anniversary to celebrate. Every day is a gift, and when walking through a life-altering loss, it tunes our hearts and minds to understand that more than ever. Don't take today for granted.

TRY THIS: PRACTICE CELEBRATING NEW (WEEKLY) MILESTONES

Start a new milestone tradition simply to practice celebrating milestones.

No matter where you find yourself on the journey, today is a place to mark a milestone of your *endurance* and progress through this time in your life.

Pick a day of the week. Any day will do. For the next month, on the day of the week you choose, permit yourself to do something special and small.

- Maybe it's having a favorite dessert with a lighted candle every Tuesday evening. The candle could be as small as a birthday candle or as large as a long taper candle.
- Another idea might be picking a special mug to drink your coffee out of on that day of the week.
- Or possibly eat your cereal out of a ridiculously large bowl every Wednesday.
- Or do your daily walk down a particular path.
- Or buy a pack of stickers to give some silliness or joy to your neighborhood barista, mail carrier, or cashier every Friday.

Whatever you pick for that day of the week, the idea is to practice enjoying the celebration of another milestone! I encourage you to make this as fun, easy, and lighthearted as possible.

Enjoy! Don't forget to celebrate for a month (at least four weeks).

FORTY
LETTING GO OF STUBBORN ANGER

"Laugh when you can, apologize when you should, and let go of what you can't change."

Author Unknown

GRIEF CAN HAVE anger attached to it. It can be turned inside, disguised as sadness. Anger in grief can be complicated, spilling into places with little to do with the circumstance. It can be displaced onto people you love and share the same grief. We, humans are masters at hiding and putting into boxes with heavy lids, things that are too painful to look at.

During my times of grief, I had to accept it in small pieces. There were days when the enormity of the loss was much too big to even look at, so I had to chew small bites at a time, swallow what I could, and try not to choke. Grief lives deep in our souls; we are never quite the same. However, it's important to make grief, especially anger, a journey and a place of passing through, not a permanent address.

If you feel plowed up by anger during your grief process, know that this is normal and your anger is valid. There are legitimate parts of loss that fuel being angry. Any type of loss can feel unfair, scary, or out of control, but in due time, the waves will smooth out, and your navigation will return. If not, don't be afraid to seek some professional assistance. Healing takes bravery and, many times, help from someone else.

God created us with emotions, anger one of them. The first example demonstrated in scripture is found in Genesis chapter four. Brothers Cain and Able presented God with their own version of the required sacrifice. Able found favor in God's eyes, and his offering was accepted, but God rejected Cain's offering. This made Cain angry enough to kill his brother. This is the first recorded murder in the Bible.

"Cain was very angry, and his face was downcast. Then the Lord said to Cain, 'Why are you so angry? Why is your face downcast? If you do what is right, will you not be accepted? But if you do not do what is right, sin is crouching at your door; it desires to have you, but you must master it.'"

Genesis 4:5-6 NIV

The account goes on to describe how Cain tricked Able into going out to a field where the fatal attack took place. Anger can destroy. God knew of the killing and said,

---

"What have you done? Listen! Your brother's blood cries out to me from the ground."

Genesis 4:10 NIV

Cain's personal sin against God ignited a fire of hatred towards his brother; he sinned even more by killing him. I'm not saying there isn't a place for anger to flare inside us when we are wronged, disappointed, or sense injustice. Anger is certainly in our nature as an option to express or react with passion. However, God is telling us to be careful and not let our reactions or behaviors overtake who we are at our core and how we treat others.

The Bible doesn't say anger is necessarily a sin, but what we do with our anger matters to Him. God's disappointment in the Israelites resulted in God's anger and caused them to wander for 40 years. The Israelites kept sinning and disobeying Him.

God often told Moses, who was leading them to the promised land, that He was so angry He wanted to destroy His people. He didn't and was persuaded each time to spare them.

> *"So the Lord was very angry with Israel and removed them from His presence."*
>
> 2 Kings 17:18 NIV

God's anger shouldn't be confused with human expression of anger. We know that God cannot sin. His anger is righteous, unlike ours. We need to keep in mind why God gets angry. Anger isn't in God, but He can show wrath when sin provokes it.

> *"Remember this and never forget how you aroused the anger of the LORD your God in the wilderness. From the day you left Egypt until you arrived here, you have been rebellious against the LORD."*
>
> Deuteronomy 9:7 NIV

How does God want us to handle anger?

James gives us one solution: be a quick listener, be slow to give our opinions and be slow to become angry. (James 1:19-20, NIV) Another solution Paul gives,

---

"Do not let the sun go down while you are still angry."

Ephesians 4:26 NIV

Scripture isn't as much saying 'don't get angry' but sharing that anger has a place, a beginning, and a time to release it. The sun goes down on one day but rises again to bring a fresh beginning—a new start to a new day.

Some of us may need to release a particular anger many times every day before the sun goes down. Don't think that releasing anger once is all that is required. Grief has a way of bringing up stubborn anger that's harder to resolve.

"Then Peter came to Jesus and asked,' Lord, how many times shall I forgive my brother when he sins against me? Up to seven times?' Jesus answered, 'I tell you, not seven times, but seventy-seven times.'"

Matthew 19:21-22 NIV

If this reading today finds you angry or feeling stirred up inside, take it to Jesus and ask Him to trade those feelings and thoughts with peace and patience. Don't let the sun go down on them.

TRY THIS: PHYSICAL MOVEMENT

The emotion of anger trapped inside can feel heavy and make us feel slow or like we want to punch a wall. Regardless of your current mood, today is a day to move.

One way to do this is to take a brisk walk. Feel the steps and lengthen your stride for short bursts. You don't need to run or jog but stretch your steps. Go outside if possible. Otherwise, a living room or garage works anywhere with space for movement. Feel your legs move. Swing your arms if you like. God has given us bodies that were designed to move.

Suppose walking is not something you can do today. Lift your body up and down. Take turns stretching out wide and scrunching in. Do this until you feel ever so slightly different.

A friend suggested a technique to dispel anger that worked better than punching a pillow. She described "twisting a towel." Taking both ends of a towel and twisting it into the tightest size you can, then releasing and doing it again has surprising anger release ability.

Pro-tip: I've found that praise music will lift my heart to a place of worship and make my soul glad!

FORTY-ONE
SUFFICIENT GRACE

"If you can't fly then run, if you can't run than walk, if you can't walk then crawl, but whatever you do you have to keep moving forward."

Martin Luther King, Jr.

THE ONLY AWARD I ever won in school was 'Most Improved in Gym.' I kid you not.

I was never on a sports team and still don't like running or jogging. I tried my hand at tennis but could never remember the score. (What's a love?!) Kickball was a favorite, but playing opportunities as a grandmother are slim.

Even though my dad was a professional basketball coach, I never considered myself a person of physical strength or athleticism.

What I did discover was that my inner strength grew. It began small and grew mighty over time. It's a good bet that this was the same for you, too. Regardless of your proximity to suffering, developing inner strength requires significant effort.

> *"Experience is a hard teacher because she gives the test first, the lesson afterward."*
>
> Vernon Law

Those who grieve are repeatedly given the test of suffering and subsequent lessons. No matter how much advance warning is provided, there's no studying for these tests. The good news is that suffering is an open-book exam. However, it still requires going *through* the grief. What we learn from grieving happens after each moment of suffering.

For our family, these "tests of suffering" continued. We were still reeling from the sudden death of our youngest, my son. At that time, my daughter was a young teenager, when we learned of my husband's cancer diagnosis. This was Round 2 for our little family. We were hit hard again.

Every medical announcement felt like riding a rollercoaster of George's various treatments, transfusions, chemotherapy, blood count results, and eventually each "milestone" of his steady decline; these were each a test of suffering. Lessons from each test soon followed, deep lessons only learned through experience. These included how to endure, how to live every minute, how to accept, how to care for each other, and how to stay hopeful.

Our family could not have learned these lessons any other way, and I am *still* pained to say that because grief never goes away completely. And yet, because those lessons were learned, we can now apply them to other areas of life.

Loss is quite a teacher. She exposes strengths and highlights weaknesses with a red marker. We are wise to take notice of both. Coping strengths get blown up with the air of survival mode. That lasts for a time but will slowly deflate unless more everlasting breath is exchanged.

> *"The Spirit of God has made me; the breath of the Almighty gives me life."*
>
> Job 33:4 NIV

God and His presence inside you give the breadth of fortitude, even when you don't understand and can't imagine going on. That's where the strength to endure suffering or loss becomes empowered. It's not from our weak, broken inner strength but from His wisdom and capacity to fill us with the ability to take one step at a time along rocky, difficult roads.

Paul, one of the most prolific writers of scripture, suffered from an undisclosed ailment. He prayed and pleaded with God to take his suffering from him.

> *"But He said to me, 'My grace is sufficient for you, for my power is made perfect in weakness.' Therefore, I will boast all the more gladly about my weakness, so that Christ's power may rest on me."*
>
> 2 Corinthians 12:9 NIV

God allowed Paul's affliction to persist, to show firsthand His ability to sustain and provide whatever was necessary to endure suffering. God's strength was most evident in the Apostle Paul when he displayed his human weaknesses. This is a promise for us as well.

Our weaknesses or afflictions are made strong as God's strength is demonstrated to us and through us. This is a powerful method to endure our tests of suffering. God loves you so much. He wants to help carry the burden that has broken you. Give it to Him and see what happens.

TRY THIS: JOURNALING ACTIVITY

On my dresser, I have a smooth, round rock I found while walking one day. It's about the size of my fist, and it found its way into my pocket for some reason. When discovered, it seemed the perfect spot to write the four words God was trying to teach me. So written in black marker on my rock is the reminder, "Alone Weak Made Strong" 2015. I often look at my stone as a physical reminder that God knew I was alone and that He was making me stronger in my weaknesses. He was and still is my rock.

Today's Journal Prompt: What is the message you want to give yourself? Or is God trying to teach you a specific message? What would you write on your rock?

Better yet, find yourself a stone and write that message as a reminder of where you are now.

FORTY-TWO
TELLING YOUR STORY

"You can't go back and change the beginning, but you can start where you are and change the ending."

C.S. Lewis

THIS HAS BEEN QUITE a week of remembering. It might have caused some painful memories, tears, and hopefully encouragement.

Earlier this week, we discussed milestones and markers that make something notable. For you, this might be a date, an event, an accomplishment, or an advancement. It could be as simple as a circumstance where you were brave and did something hard or a day to remember for whatever reason.

We need milestones to help keep in mind noteworthy times or events. A wedding is certainly a milestone event; a new role is established, and a frame is put around a couple's relationship.

Milestones can mark hard events, too—the anniversary date of a death, an accident, or a loss.

Just the other day would've been my son's birthday. I've been celebrating his birthday for 38 years, even though he died when he was nine years old. Even this many years into grief, I can tell you that it keeps spilling out from all sides of life.

I took myself to a restaurant that I knew he would've liked. I sat down in my booth, and an unexpected well of tears thinking about Mark appeared out of nowhere. The server asked me how I was, and I surprised myself when I choked up as I told her about Mark's birthday and his death.

She patted my arm and said kindly, "It's never easy." I ordered dinner, had some wine, and decided to get some cake too. The server wordlessly brought the cake with a single lit candle. This simple gesture so touched me.

Grief has a way of opening up sad places of loss, especially through unexpected gestures like a single lit candle. Yes, we grieve the loss of a source of joy, and yes, we can choose new sources of joy as well—a simple piece of cake with a single lit candle.

So there I am, sitting in a booth, feeling a little blue, when the check arrives for $12. I waved my server over and asked why the bill listed such a significant discount. She and her boss decided to help me celebrate and gave me my entree and dessert on the house. On top of the lit candle, this additional gesture prompted tears to well up.

I had to simply sit in the booth for a little bit, quietly crying, missing my little boy.

It was not a pity party. It was a grief party: messy, a little bit all over the place, hard to contain, with lots of feelings, and cake.

Had I not been alone, this celebration would've been overshadowed by other people and conversations. Instead, it was just reminiscing, allowing my focus to land on the story of his life, his death, and my loss. As a result, now, there is an opportunity to share it with those who need it.

Don't let your reminiscing or celebration be overshadowed. Sometimes, this might look like a fear of letting go and picking up the new thing life offers you. Even if you think your life will never be as happy, fulfilling, or productive, I encourage you to shift your focus to the blessings that might result from this new thing.

Find ways to celebrate. Celebrate your story, your journey, and your strength. Your strength and growing faith are an inspiration to someone else, and just maybe that's the point. God doesn't waste anything. He will use you and what you've walked through to help someone you might not even know yet.

Celebrating your strength is one of many ways we crawl out of "the thick of it." There is always someone a few steps behind you that can be encouraged by your bravery and overcoming challenges.

Finally, don't leave God and your growing faith out of the recipe of your life. He really is the binding ingredient that holds all things together.

What a great 6-weeks these have been together. I've enjoyed imagining you, praying the hard days you are experiencing now will be used for a purpose, even if you don't see that now. I sit beside you across the page and am thankful for you as a fellow hiker through grief.

Keep going.

You can make it through these confusing times. Hopefully, you found comfort in reading the words of my story and will be able to comfort someone with yours.

TRY THIS: A RECIPE — SLOPPY JOE'S

To honor the shared messiness of grief and all the reminiscence covered from this week's readings, here's a long-time favorite family recipe for Sloppy Joe's Sandwiches.

My father was a small northern college basketball coach and athletic director. On the nights of his games, my mom would make a big batch of this yummy stove-top-drippy dish and serve it on soft toasted buttered buns. It was a quick dinner for a big family so we could head out to cheer for the Purple Knights, Dad's team. Truth be told, I loved this dinner almost more than watching his team play!

Sloppy Joe's

Serves 6

Ingredients

- 1 tablespoon of olive oil
- ½ medium onion chopped, medium bell pepper chopped
- 1 pound ground beef
- 1 cup ketchup
- 1 tablespoon of Worcestershire sauce
- 1 tablespoon of brown sugar
- 1 tablespoon of yellow mustard
- 1 tablespoon of apple cider vinegar
- Pinch of red pepper flakes (optional)
- 6 hamburger buns, soft butter-to-toast buns
- Optional: The perfect side dish is potato chips. :-)

Directions

1. Combine ketchup, Worcestershire sauce, Brown sugar, yellow mustard, and apple cider vinegar into a small bowl.
2. Heat the pan to medium-high heat, and add olive oil. Add chopped onion and bell pepper and sauté until soft, not mushy.
3. Remove vegetables from the pan and add ground beef. I like adding a little butter to the pan to flavor the browning meat. Break up into small pieces to brown nicely. Dab out the grease with paper towels if necessary. Add back onion and pepper.
4. Pour the contents of the bowl into the meat mixture. Simmer for 10–15 minutes.
5. Taste to ensure the salt and pepper, ketchup, brown sugar, and

mustard flavors are bright enough for your liking. Adjust if necessary.

6. Butter the buns and toast butter side down in a pan. Top with warm Sloppy Joe mixture and, of course, serve with tater tots or potato chips. *ENJOY!*

APPENDIX

GROUP GUIDE FOR FINDING THE MEANING OF GRIEF

When the writing of *Finding The Meaning of Grief* was complete, getting the finishing touches in place, it occurred to me someone might want to use this book with a group and go through the pages together.

What kind of groups?

Book clubs, grief groups, therapy groups, bible study groups, church small groups, neighborhood hangouts, or even a friend or two make a great reason to go through a book like this together.

The meeting format can be anything you decide. Some groups might want to make it a potluck and bring one of the **Recipes**. The recipes are a great way to add another layer of sharing and community to a group setting. Food has always been a way to include others in a circle of community. Grief is a time to make room at your table or be brave enough to include yourself with other people.

Some groups might want to do one or two **Try This** activities together. The book's outline is loose enough for the group to use the week's readings and activities as they seem the best and most helpful. It might be fun to do a writing prompt together and share the words that come out during your time together.

Other groups might want just to talk or use the **Group Questions** provided below to bolster discussion.

Why a group?

Community is so healing, no matter how fresh or stale your grief might be. Your group may be as small as one other person you feel comfortable sharing this season of grief with. Your group might meet to comfort and support each other. My hope is that if you use this book in your group, you will use it to aid in your group's encouragement, community, and sharing. I'm excited to see how the book can spark outreach to others who may be suffering alone.

PS - Send me an email (visit jhaney.com). I might be able to show up at one of your group meetings via video conference to say hello!

WEEKLY GROUP QUESTIONS

Whenever you get together, here are ten questions that might be good to ask one another (in no particular order):

1. Was there anything in the reading or activities that surprised you?
2. Which day's reading impacted you the most?
3. Was anything harder or more difficult than you imagined? (i.e., hard to read, hard to do)
4. How does your situation relate or not relate to this week's reading?
5. How might your life be altered from this week's activities? How might someone else's?
6. What does your grief feel like today?
7. What is something positive you're seeing in someone else's grief journey?
8. What does "finding meaning in grief" look like for you this week?
9. If you could put a voice to the changes happening in your life, what would that voice say?
10. What is grief teaching or showing you?

MORE TOOLS & ACTIVITIES

HERE ARE a few more suggestions for activities to try. These are in addition to or in the palace of the offerings at the end of every day's reading. Sometimes, more options to choose from is a good idea.

Mason Jars & Popsicle Sticks

Creating this jar might take a little time at first, but you can keep it ready when your grief feels a little too heavy or when you need Godly encouragement.

1 Gather your favorite scriptures.

◦ *See the More Comfort Scripture section for some of my favorites.*

2 Jot down the scripture reference on a slip of paper or popsicle sticks, one for each verse, and drop them into a jar.

3 Pick out one scripture "address" and look it up in the Bible.

4 Write out the verse across the top of an empty piece of paper.

5 Take a moment to consider what the Lord is saying through the verse and saying to you on that day.

6 Then start writing or journaling!

- Don't worry about spelling, editing your content, or saving your words forever— just follow wherever your words take you.

Dice Up Your Decisions

This is for the days when you're feeling overwhelmed but have some tasks that require attention. It's also a good one to do when life feels way too serious and needs a little levity or a small morsel of fun.

1 Find a 6-sided die

- Borrow one from a board game!

2 Make a list of at least six tasks that are overwhelming you or need to be done today (no more than six tasks)

- Tip: If a "task" takes longer than 15 minutes, divide it into two or more tasks.

3 Assign each task a number 1 through 6

4 Roll the dice once.

5 Whatever number appears, do that numbered task on your list.

- Optional: After completing a task, replace it with something else (e.g., just in case you roll a 6 four times).

6 Roll the die as many times as you like

7 Congratulate yourself for outsourcing today's decisions.

8 Feel accomplished.

30 in 30 Challenge (Friends & Family Edition!)

This is a fun way to keep the circle of important people close during your season of grief, no matter how far away they may be.

1 List the 30 most important people in your life—friends, family, 3rd cousins twice-removed, colleagues, college roommates, etc.

2 Connect with a different person every day for 30 days—postcards, phone calls, emails, social media, writing a prayer, etc.

3 Helpful Tip: Use your list of family and friends in your calendar, one person each day.

If the 30-in-30 Challenge seems too daunting, you can use this list of family and friends combined with your personal calendar as a reminder to pray for each person or reach out to them as inspired.

Set the Timer

Feel one singular emotion for five *full* minutes. It's harder than you think!

Dig in the Dirt

Backyard or potted plants, or volunteer at a local park or nursing home to weed the community garden. Buy a plant, grow something.

Bring Comfort Outside

Sunshine has been documented to have more benefits than you think. It's a natural source of vitamin D and helps our body inside and out. Just a few minutes of sun exposure can help with sleep and mood.

1 Bring something you find comforting from *indoors* (cup of coffee, quilt, etc.) to spend some time *outdoors*.

◦ Your local park might have a covered picnic shelter area even if it's raining.

◦ Hack: This can be as easy as sitting on your front steps.

2 Set the timer for a length that feels doable for today.

3 People watch, car watch, bird watch, cloud watch, or bug hunt.

4 Notice how your mood changes.

MORE WRITING PROMPTS

JOURNALING IS a place to collect your thoughts and emotions on paper. Discovering what's been swirling around inside your head or heart is often a surprise. Even feelings left dormant and unnoticed have a place to come to light.

There are spaces to journal or jot down your reaction in *Finding The Meaning of Grief*. However, having a specific journal or notebook to privately write the words that spring from your heart and mind is very helpful. Often, I don't want my emotions to be 'public' in the volume of a book. If that's you, and you are new to the idea of journaling, any notebook will work. Remember to date your entries to track where your life, thoughts, and emotions take you and when. That way, you can watch for patterns and insights or just remember the season in which your writing took place.

Below are some journaling prompts from the pages of my book titled *Write Your Way Through Change: a 21-day Devotional for Grief and Major Life Transitions*

If journaling or writing your thoughts is something you enjoy, please take the opportunity to use some of the following prompts to get your pen moving.

Here are a few prompts taken from *Write Your Way Through Change*

1. Life is full of hills and valleys and an occasional meadow. Even the treacherous mountains we must climb have a purpose if we look for it. What have you discovered about how to live your life well from the trials and pitfalls you have traveled?
2. Do you think that your hard times created who you are today? Do accumulated difficulties lead to wisdom? How so? Or Why not?
3. Describe a time when God answered a prayer of desperation in your life. Looking back, did the answer strengthen your faith in trusting God more? If so, how so?
4. It's easy to pile up excuses or find blame as to why a particular thing has or has not happened. Being as honest as possible, write about an excuse that stopped you from doing something you wanted.
5. Do you see yourself on a particular stepping-stone in thinking of the change you are going through now? Are you on the Letting Go Stone? Are you on the Middle Stepping Stone? Have you made it to the New Thing Stone?
6. Initially, problems might make us want to give up. On average, which is true for you, does a problem light a fire to keep trying harder, or do you lay down a difficulty and sit on it for a while? Write about an example.
7. Have you ever thought of your life as a story to tell? It is, and it's worthy of the telling. Start here and share an account of who you are and why. Someone needs to hear it.
8. Are there times in your life when you rocked the boat? What was the outcome?

Here are additional journal prompts to consider and help with your journaling process.

Finish These Sentences

Another way to encourage thoughts lost in your mind or heart and get them onto paper is a prompt to finish a sentence. Reading the line, see what comes to mind. Write about it. It might be a single word or fill an entire page. The thoughts and emotions that need expression might just surprise you.

1. Today, I miss...
2. Today, I remember...
3. If you were here with me, I'd tell you...
4. I'm having a difficult time with...
5. Today, the grief feels like a...
6. The grief is settling in my body today, and it feels like...
7. I need more...
8. I want more...
9. I need less...
10. I want less...
11. Now I fill my time with...
12. I want my friends/family to know...
13. I wish my friends/family could...
14. Because I no longer can, I'm now able to...
15. Today, kindness and comfort look like...
16. Grief has surprised/shocked me when...
17. If grief was a rollercoaster...

A Moment in Time

This journaling technique takes the writer to a place in time as if looking at a photograph. A recent mental snapshot can be as compelling as one from years ago. The moment captured can be as small as a remembered smile or as life-changing as your child's birth.

A Moment in Time is just that, a memory that marks you. This writing technique calls upon all the senses, sight, smell, touch, or sound, present at that particular moment. The point is to capture the moment fully with as much awareness as possible.

Think of a moment—a sunset at the beach, the smile of your granddaughter, the touch of holding your partner's hand, your first kiss, the moment you heard the "news," a swim at the lake, getting your driver's license, a broken plate... the moment to remember can be anything and not necessarily attached to grief. It can be joy-filled or hilarious, tiny and unremarkable at the time. There's no limit.

When a moment comes to mind, start writing it down. Use as much description as possible. Think of all the angles, spaces, and rooms this memory has surrounding it. This technique can bring you to an awareness you might not have noticed then, and that's the point.

Recapture a moment in time.

I Wish

List six things you wish for

1.

2.

3.

4.

5.

6.

Pick one of your wishes and write about what you would do if granted. How would you be affected?

Loss

Grief is born from loss. What areas of your life have been touched by your loss? Be specific and describe the areas in as much detail as possible.

Journal prompt: My grief has touched…..

Then answer the next question: Is there any part of you or your life that grief has **not** touched? Have you insulated yourself from the pain? Are there parts of your life or self unaffected by the loss?

Journal Prompt: My grief has **not** touched…..

. . .

The Feeling

Grief unleashes many layers of feelings. The spectrum is wide and deep. In the early days, numbness becomes a feeling, and even simple decisions become impossible. Rage, panic, emptiness, physical pain, depression, isolation, acting out, and short-temperedness are emotional reactions to the feelings grief wakes up.

Write about *The Feeling*. What has been stirred up inside your heart that needs a place to unload? Journaling is a safe place to do just that.

Journal Prompt: The Feeling is…

A Time to Listen

Listening is a skill. It takes time and effort. To be a listener, one must hear what the other person is saying or explaining. God wants us to be listeners. He speaks to us in times of suffering in many ways. We can hear Him if we listen. It might not be through a booming voice or a parting of waters, but He speaks to the brokenhearted in soft, healing ways. God provides His touch through a friend sitting silently beside you, giving sunshine to warm your face, sharing a verse that touches your soul, and sending someone to give you a hug and a shoulder at the right moment. Listen for these touches from God, who knows what you need.

Here are the ways I can listen for the ways God will speak to me. What is God saying to me today?

1.

2.

3.

4.

Write a Letter

DEAR _____,
I JUST WANTED TO TELL YOU...

Triggers

What triggers the following emotions? Write as much explanation as you need.

- What triggers Happiness?
- What triggers Fear?
- What triggers Joy?
- What triggers Forgiveness?
- What triggers peace?
- What triggers Anger?
- What triggers love
- What triggers Safety?
- What triggers pain?
- What triggers Laughter?

MORE SCRIPTURES FOR HOPE

THERE MIGHT BE a day that shows up when you need a special word from the Lord and don't know where to look. I've listed a few of my favorite Scriptures for those days. Take these and tuck them into your heart for just such a time. They make a great journal prompt and become a sticky note blessing on a bathroom mirror. As you find Scriptures of your own, list ones important to you. These are like stepping stones across the wild waters whose grief stirs up. They give a solid place to stand and something outside yourself to hold on to.

If you don't have a Bible, contact me through my website, and I'll gladly send you one; jhaney.com

"Strengthen the feeble hands, steady the knees that give way. Say to those with fearful hearts, 'be strong, do not fear; your God will come with vengeance; with divine retribution He will come to save you.'" Isaiah 35:3-4 NIV

"Have I not commanded you? Be strong and courageous. Do not be terrified; do not be discouraged, for the Lord your God will be with you wherever you go." Joshua 1:9 NIV

"If you falter in times of trouble, how small is your strength!" Proverbs 24:10 NIV

"But those who hope in the Lord will renew their strength. They will soar on wings like eagles; they will run and not grow weary, they will walk and not be faint." Isaiah 40:31 NIV

"You arm me with strength for the battle; you make my adversaries bow at my feet." Psalm 18:39 NIV

"If the Lord delights in a man's way, he makes his steps firm; though he stumbles, he will not fall, for the Lord upholds him with His hand." Psalm 37:23-24 NIV

"Do not be anxious about anything, but in everything, by prayer and petition, with thanksgiving, present your request to God. And the peace of God, which transcends all understanding, will guard your hearts and your mind" Philippians 4:6-7 NIV

"I can do everything through Him who gives me strength." Philippians 4:13 NIV

"Love the Lord your God with all your heart and with all your soul and with all your strength." Deuteronomy 6:5 NIV

"Be strong and courageous. Do not be afraid or terrified because of them, for the Lord your God goes with you; He will never leave you nor forsake you." Deuteronomy 31:6 NIV

"Look to the Lord and His strength; seek His face always." 1 Chronicles 16:11 NIV

"So do not fear, for I am with you; do not be dismayed, for I am your God. I will strengthen you and help you; I will uphold you with my righteous right hand." Isaiah 41:10 NIV

"My dear brothers, take note of this: Everyone should be quick to listen, slow to speak and slow to become angry. For a person's anger does not bring about the righteous life that God desires." James 1:19-20 NIV

"Let the morning me word of your unfailing love, for I have put my trust in you. Show me the way I should go, for to You, I lift up my soul." Psalm 143:8 NIV

"I waited patiently for the Lord; he turned to me and heard my cry, He lifted me out of the slimy pit, out of the mud and mire; he set my feet on a rock and gave me a firm place to stand. He put a new song in my mouth, a hymn of praise to our God. Many will see and fear and put their trust in the Lord." Psalm 40:1-3 NIV

"My tears have been my food day and night, while men say to me all day long, 'Where is your God?' Why are you so downcast, O my soul? Why so disturbed within me? Put your hope in God, for I will yet praise Him my Savior and my God." Psalm 42: 3, 5 NIV

"Those who sow in tears will reap with songs of joy." Psalm 126:5 NIV

"I consider that our present sufferings are not worth comparing with the glory that will be revealed in us." Romans 8:18 NIV

"Consider it pure joy, my brothers, whenever you face trials of many kinds, because you know that the testing of your faith develops perseverance. Perseverance must finish its work so that you may be natural and complete, but not lacking anything." James 1:2-4 NIV

"The Lord is close to the brokenhearted and saves those who are crushed in spirit. A righteous man may have many troubles, but the Lord delivers him from them all; he protects all his bones, not one of them will be broken." Psalm 34:18-19 NIV

"See, I have engraved you on the palms of my hands; your walls are ever before me." Isaiah 49:16 NIV

"Yet this I call to mind, and therefore I have hope: because of the Lord's great love we are not consumed, for His compassions never fail. They are new every morning; great is your faithfulness. I say to myself, 'The lord is my portion; therefore I will wait for Him.'" Lamentations 3:21-24 NIV

"See, I am doing a new thing! Now it springs up; do you not perceive it? I am making a way in the desert and streams in the wasteland." Isaiah 43:18-19 NIV

"Jesus answered, 'I am the way and the truth and the life. No one comes to the Father except through me." John 14:27 NIV

"What, then, shall we say in response to this? If God is for us, who can be against us?" Romans 8:31 NIV

RECOMMENDED READING

I've collected this list of books that spoke to me at various points along my grief journey.

In the early days, in the deepest shock of grief, I couldn't bring myself to read. My concentration wasn't there, and the words seemed to melt off the page and drop to the floor. Actually, I don't have many of those early grief books. One day, in a flash of anger, I threw them away.

When I was ready to read again, I started a new collection and have kept them on my shelf to reread and share with others.

So, no matter where you are in grief, feel free to keep and share this list. Moments will arrive when you need to be encouraged, embrace some joy, hear another person's grief story or need help reaching out. Please know each one has touched my heart in some way or another. You might find a few to touch yours as well.

Happy Reading!

~ *Janet*

SHAMELESS PLUGS

- *Hello Nobody: Standing at the Door Alone, What to Do When Everything Changes*, By Janet Haney (ISBN 9781535293655) This is my story. After the losses in my life, I came home one day from work and called out to a now empty house, "Hello nobody…" I knew that was the start of a journey to tell my story of how I coped when everything changed.

- *Write Your Way Through Change: A 21-day Devotional Journal for Grief and Major Life Transitions*, By Janet Haney (ISBN 9 78099 729441) Along my grief journey, I realized how much journaling helped me. Some days, the page was filled with a single word written 60 times. My heart poured out on other days, and I couldn't write my thoughts fast enough. Some days, I stared at a blank page before shutting the journal; I had nothing to give the page. I decided a way to help other grief sufferers' journals was to provide thoughts and prompts to give a framework and a designated place to unload thoughts, feelings, fears, anger, and the sadness grief unleashes. So, this book was born.

- *Bare Naked Bravery: How to Be Creatively Courageous*, by Emily Ann Peterson (Editor of this book!) I never thought of myself as brave, but having Emily Ann Peterson in my book-writing corner has helped me realize that bravery is possible for everyone, no matter how small it starts. I recommend her book as a place to start if you need to understand what bravery looks like and want to develop it for yourself. This is a book everyone needs on their shelf to read, regardless of where you happen to be on your life journey. Bravery is an inner confidence that can be taught and practiced, becoming an important framework for moving forward from any hardship. I am braver and more resilient, understanding how courage is possible. My copy of *Bare Naked Bravery* is underlined, and the pages are dog-eared. I'm sure you will find your copy to be as loved as mine.

GRIEF & FAITH

- *When God Doesn't Fix It: Lessons You Never Wanted to Learn, Truths You Can't Live Without*, by Laura Story. (ISBN 97907 18 036973) I picked up this book after George died, intrigued by the title, because God certainly didn't fix cancer for me. My husband was gone. Despite the pain in my own heart, I was encouraged by Laura's story and sat beside her through every page as she encountered the tragic medical illness of her husband. God may not "fix" everything as we ask for. He can teach us how to live with broken dreams. In a well-written way, this book lets me observe someone else's grief journey, all while traveling on my own.

- *Grieving With Hope: Finding Comfort as You Journey Through Loss*, by Samuel J. Hodges IV and Kathy Leonard (ISBN 978-0-8010-1423-9) The authors of this book know grief and what it does to you. The chapters are short yet packed with information about grief. It's written as a guide, offering stepping stones of information about grief and helping a person navigate. The book is divided topically, so it's a good one to pick up if you're only in the mood for one chapter at a time. I found the insights helpful regarding what to expect throughout grief and how to have hope while making the journey.

- *A Grief Observed: Reader's Edition* By C.S. Lewis (ISBN 978-0-571-31087-6) After our little boy died, this was the book my husband George read multiple times over. His grief was put to words by the writing of C.S. Lewis. The book describes Lewis's powerful struggle between inconsolable grief and the struggle to keep his faith. It is a brilliantly accurate account of how the depths of grief can consume. Lewis successfully gave voice to millions of hearts going through the bereavement process. If there were a book considered to be a "classic" on grief, this would certainly be a top contender. (Fun fact: It was originally published under the pseudonym; "N.W.Clerk," masking the identity of the true author, C.S. Lewis. It wasn't until after his death (1898-1963) that the estate permitted the book to be published with the correct author identified.)

- *Keep a Quiet Heart*, By Elizabeth Elliot (ISBN 0-89283-906-6) The collection of writings in this book are articles that were featured in Elizabeth Elliot's newsletter. Each writing is short, two pages or so, and makes for good reading when concentrating on a longer chapter seems too much. This is the kind of book that's easy to pick up and land on a reading selection that seems to just "hit the spot." It is not necessarily a book from a grief perspective; it is more of a collection of articles that touch on themes we all face, including loss, love, faith, family, pain, peace, and finding quiet. Her book encourages a reader to seek quiet places where we can know God more deeply. When I picked up this book from my shelf to add to this list, I was surprised to find so many dog-eared pages that marked spots where Elliot's well-crafted words had touched me. I think you will discover your own pages of impact.

- *The Problem of Pain*, By C.S. Lewis (ISBN 978-0-06-065296-8) If you've been asking questions like, "If God is good and all-powerful, then why does he allow his creatures to suffer pain?" then this might be a good book for you to have on hand. Lewis doesn't intend to give answers to the grieving process but lays out the argument of how God uses pain for our good. He doesn't dismiss that pain hurts, but it has a purpose. Lewis is a most extraordinary writer. No surprise, his thoughts are deep and profound.

- *The Problem of Pain: A Bible Study on the C.S. Lewis Book The Problem of Pain*, By Alan Vermilye (ISBN 9781948481021) This is a 10-chapter workbook that breaks down each chapter of the book by C.S. Lewis for group or individual study. I found it an excellent way to dig into the depths of *The Problem of Pain*, which can be a bit intellectually heavy. Vermilye offers word definitions and a full summary of each chapter; he even includes the answers to the questions asked in the study. The well-detailed plan of this workbook opens up the powerful message Lewis offers in his book.

- *Experiencing Grief*, H. Norman Wright (ISBN 978-0-8054-3092-9) This is a short read but a mighty one. It seeks to explain the normality and the process grief takes. The twenty small chapters encourage that your grief is 'normal,' a good thing to know when feeling anything but normal. I've given this book as a gift to fellow grief sufferers. Its small size is not overwhelming, and in my early days of loss, I needed just that.

- *Recovering from Losses in Life*, H. Norman Wright (ISBN 978-0-80007-3155-7) As a certified trauma counselor, H. Norman Wright comes through with another powerful book about loss. This book explains how to keep walking through the loss now in your life. My copy is underlined and marked up. I recommend reading it with a highlighter, as its insights are helpful and ones you'll want to remember.

- *Dark Clouds Deep Mercy: Discovering the Grace of Lament*, By Mark Vroegop (ISBN 978-1-4335-6148-1) We don't hear the word lament much in conversation circles; however, we have experienced it. Defined as "a passionate expression of deep sorrow," we know it well. Biblically, lament is found in the Psalms or the book of Lamentations, and Vroegop shows us how to lament and the benefits of doing so. This book gives permission to look at our deep sorrow and pain and even includes a worksheet to express the suffering through scripture. I like how the book teaches bringing our sorrow to God.

- *Good Grief,* by Granger E Westberg (ISBN 978-0-8006-9781-5) When this small, purse-size book was printed, in 2011, the cover boasted 'more than 3 million sold'. It could be another 3 million have sold to date, as this go-to pocket-size gem has much to offer a person grieving. Westberg gives permission to be honest in grieving and explains that is the pathway to making it through. He offers ten grief stages that help categorize the feelings that grief ushers in. The framework to know what to expect helps cope with the unearthed emotion grief unleashes.

- *Conquering the Mysteries and Lies of Grief, Second Edition, by Sherry Russell (ISBN 9-7809-84-059508)* A while back, I took a class called Journal Through Grief. This recommendation was the textbook assigned to the class. Of course, my copy has been read many times since taking the course and is highlighted and underlined. I was well acquainted with loss and grief at the time of the class, but I appreciated how this book led us through the stages and variables that made grief unique to each of us.

- *Suffering: Gospel Hope When Life Doesn't Make Sense*, By Paul David Tripp. (ISBN 978-1-4335-5677-7) This book is a favorite of mine to read and give to others. Of all my books on walking through grief, this is the one I give away the most. I even led a small group at my church using this book. Tripp's story of his suffering is captivating, and his struggle is real. He writes from a place of truth because his life was turned upside down. He shares the traps of grief and the hope and comfort God provides during these times of suffering. I highly recommend this book to read and to share.

- **Suffering: Eternity Makes a Difference** By Paul David Tripp (ISBN 978-87552-684-3) This is a 31-page booklet by Tripp, the same author of the book *Suffering: Gospel Hope When Life Doesn't Make Sense.* As a small and pocket-size resource, I have turned to this booklet when encouraging a new grief sufferer. It provides faith-based information in a bite-size form. It is from the Changing Lives Series, which has many other small booklets on any number of topics, including anger, forgiveness, anger at God, depression, self-injury, suicide, why me, or priorities, just to name a few. See all the booklets for the Changing Lives series at www.prpbooks.com

- *Hope for the Brokenhearted: God's Voice of Comfort in the Midst of Grief and Loss*, By Dr. John Luke Terveen (ISBN 978-078 1443623) This book tells the story of the death of a 14-year-old daughter from the eyes of her Dad. In his grieving, he searched more than 200 books on grief, not finding the comfort he was looking for. He discovered that the Bible was the greatest source of comfort, and all the other books he scoured didn't match up. I have this book on both my Kindle and in paperback.

- *The Book of Comforts: Genuine Encouragement for Hard Times*, by Faires, Faires, Wernt and Wilder (ISBN 978-0-310-45206-5) This is more like a coffee table book--a good book to keep or to give--one to pick up, leaf through the pretty pages until your heart lands on just the place of comfort you are looking for. The authors describe their book as being born around a dinner table, each allowing themselves to share the grief inside broken hearts. (Tip: If you or someone you know is responsible for maintaining the reading selections for the waiting room in a doctor or dentist's office, this book is a universally applicable comfort to keep on hand.)

BOOKS THAT ENCOURAGE JOURNALING

- *Progressing Through Grief: Guided Exercises to Understand Your Emotions and Recover From Loss, By Stephanie Jose (ISBN 978-1-62315-722-7)* This book gives permission to feel your grief and explains that grieving doesn't completely end; it "evolves and becomes integrated into your life." Jose uses the tool of journaling in this book to help give you a place to document your unique journey into a loss. She gives space inside the book to answer prompt questions and have room to write your own journal entries.

- *Writing Out the Storm: Reading and Writing Your Way Through Serious Illness or Injury, By Barbara Abercrombie (ISBN 0-312-28545-0)* I picked up this book when I was going through my own bout with breast cancer. I wanted a read that would be encouraging and supportive without being too "rah-rah-you-can-do-this-because-I-have." I just wanted someone to encourage me to write what I felt then. Her own journey through breast cancer gave me someone I could travel next to without being smothered. I had my own trials to navigate. This was a book I sent to my sister-in-law when she was diagnosed with breast cancer. Even though she's not a journaler or writer, just thinking about the questions posed helps to untie the knots in your mind that form when serious illness strikes.

- *Writing As A Way of Healing: How Telling Our Stories Transforms Our Lives,* By Louise DeSalvo (ISBN 978-0-8070-7243-1) This is another book that allows the reader to discover the healing power of writing, but not just any writing. Her research explains that the 'right' kind of writing can be very restorative. This book is underlined and dog-eared from my reading. Unlike other books about writing to explore grief, this is not a grief journal. The author doesn't give writing space and includes much reading about the writing process. The insight and information are very helpful and encourage writing with purpose.

- *The Artist Way: A Spiritual Path to Higher Creativity, A Course in Discovering and Recovering Your Creative Self,* By Julia Cameron (ISBN 978-1-58542-146-6) This book takes the reader on a 12-week journey that will change how you see yourself and the world around you. She believes everyone is born with creativity, and it's possible to awaken that sleeping (in many people) giant. She offers two distinct, powerful activities at the core of personal discovery. These are The Morning Pages and The Artist Date. Don't be fooled by the thought that you are not an artist and this book isn't for you. You are, and it is.

- *The Artist Way: Morning Pages, A Companion Volume to The Artist Way,* By Julia Cameron (ISBN 978-0-87477-886-1) Don't be alarmed when opening this book for the first time. After reading a few pages of explanation and purpose, there are 264 blank pages. That's the point. You are to fill the empty pages each morning with your own words. The writing is to be done completely from the "top of your head," with no correcting or rereading allowed. You are just writing. You will be amazed at what pours out and what's released, even if you don't read it. Give this duo of books a try; you will be glad.

- *The Miracle Morning, The Not-So-Obvious Secret Guaranteed to Transform Your Life (Before 8 AM),* By Hal Elrod (ISBN 978-1-637744-34-5) If the above-mentioned artsy books are not your cup of tea, while not grief-centric, this book is a good one to pick up if you need a little structure in your life. After suffering a horrific car accident, Elrod is determined to rise above his circumstances. He studied what traits and habits "successful" people portrayed. Then he came up with a 6-part method that claims to transform your life, which includes things like silence, affirmations, visualization, exercise, reading, and scribing. This was exactly what my friend Max was looking for during her time of need.

NON-FICTION

- *EVERY MOMENT HOLY: Volumes 1 & 2,* By Douglas Kaine McKelvey (ISBN 978-1-951872-02-1) (ISBN 978-1-951872-09-0) I learned of these books from a friend who attended a family member's funeral. It was a tragic, sudden loss of a young mom who touched many lives. The service had over 1000 people in attendance, and her sisters read the books from these volumes. My friend who attended explained how touching and powerful the chosen readings were. So, I include *Every Moment Holy* as two small books with a big impact. I have added them to my bookshelf.

Volumes 1 and 2 are collections of beautiful liturgies for any number of different circumstances, not just for grief. These are great prayer starters, prayers themselves, quiet time readings, or just a way to encourage someone in their daily life. In Volume 1, there are readings for preparing a meal, washing windows, planting flowers, changing diapers, moving into a new home—the list goes on and on.

Liturgies in Volume 2 are filled with beautiful words for loss and grief, prayers including Those Suffering from Miscarriage, For Those Who Feel Abandoned by One who Chose Suicide, The Scattering of Ashes, Returning to Normal life After a Loss—plus many more topics. These volumes give words in the form of prayers to things that are often unspeakable or simple joys easily missed. There is a volume 3 available, but I don't have it.

- *Moving Forward After Abortion, Finding Comfort in God,* By Camille Cates (ISBN 978-1-64507-312-3) My church bought a copy of this book for every family unit. They thought someone might feel singled out and uncomfortable reaching for this book. So, the entire congregation at all three campuses was asked to take a copy. Abortion is a very personal and often life-altering experience. I stand with my church for wanting to come around women who may be hurting in this way. If that's you or you know someone, please do as my church suggested: take this book as a sign of reaching out.

- *Humble Roots: How Humility Grounds and Nourishes Your Soul* By Hannah Anderson (ISBN 978-0-8024-1459-5) This was a book club selection at my church. I remember thinking, "Sounds good for the book club, but I am pretty humble already…" Great start, huh? Boy, was I wrong. Once I allowed myself to enter the meat of this book, which started with chapter One titled "Withering on the Vine," I was hooked. This book became a very underlined, marked in the margins read that opened my eyes to parts of me I didn't realize. I also have a new understanding of what true humility is and how to practice it. The author has a gifted way of blending stories, information about plants, and God's true peace.

- *When God Writes Your Life Story: Experiencing the Ultimate Adventure,* Eric and Leslie Ludy (ISBN 1-59052-339-3) I must admit that when I picked up this book, I didn't feel very full of dreams or living an impossible life. I was just trying to make sense of the life I found myself trying to conquer after loss. But not too far into my reading, I realized how much I needed this book to change the narrative of my thinking. Eric Ludy writes of "Christ-enabled living. Impossible living. Heroic living." I needed a new direction. I hope that your impossible living thinking is awakened, as mine was.

- *Trusting God,* By Jerry Bridges (ISBN 978-1-63146-792-9) Jerry Bridges makes a good point in this book: "Why is it easier to obey God than to trust Him?" He explores this very critical question through 14 chapters and 12 lessons, followed by a Study Guide. I like a book that gives space for questions, exploration, and discussion, even if you have a dialogue with yourself. (*Psst!* This one makes a great book club as the meat of each chapter can spark questions, answers, and deeper understanding.)

• *Bittersweet: Thoughts on Change, Grace and Learning the Hard Way*, by Shauna Niequist (ISBN 978-0-310-33528-3) This book is in my personal "read again" pile at home. The title of this book says it all. Life is bittersweet. Life has many good things and times, sometimes even more hard times. Niequist has given us a glimpse into her life as her stories take us to places where we can all relate. Pick up this book when you want a short chapter to peek into the life and heart of a person living life as we all do, with hope, fear, transitions, loss, and grace.

DEVOTIONALS

- *Savor: Living Abundantly Where You Are, As You Are, 365 Devotions*, By Shauna Niequist (ISBN 978-0-310-34497-1) This is an inspiring devotional, not just for the daily writings but for the underlying message of savoring and paying greater attention to life all around you. She writes that space must be cleared away to give room to hear the drumbeat of God's voice and pay attention. She calls us to savor the day, and so we do. An added plus in this book is that she includes a recipe to make at the end of each week. Sharing time and food around the table with those you love is just as important. (100% I agree!)

- *Quiet Times for Those Who Grieve: Hope and Healing for Your Heart*, By H. Norman Wright (ISBN 978-0-7369-7107-2) This is a perfect choice when you are crashing in the middle of your pain and you want something to read but can't bring yourself to read for extended periods. Each chapter is no more than 2-4 small pages. The message is simple: comfort and hope can be found in "quiet rest," and God is sitting right there next to you, even if you can't feel Him. This book is easy to pick up and find comfort.

- ***Dark Clouds Deep Mercy: Devotional Journal,*** By Mark Vroegop (ISBN 978-1-4335-8308-7) Vroegop has written a wonderful journal to accompany the book of the same name as a stand-alone 15-day guided exercise through the Psalms of Lament. Each day, there is space to write a personal lament. I never really understood what lament was or its powerful purpose until stumbling upon Mark Vreogop's book of a similar title, *Dark Clouds Deep Mercy Discovering the Grace of Lament* (also on this list). This accompanying journal volume takes a reader by the hand and gives an explanation and space to write your own laments. Each of the 15 Psalms used for reflection in the journal includes an Outline Sheet, which guides the reader into a deeper examination of the Psalm. In reading over the marked pages of my copy of the journal, I'm struck by the insight into my grief that emerged in my following the prompts and answering the questions. This is a great book to keep or to give to another person trying to walk through their own grief.

- ***Give Me 40 Days: An Invitation for an Encounter With God,*** By Freeda Bowers (ISBN 0-88270-856-2) Flipping through the pages of this devotional takes me back to some hard days. The year I read this book, George had only one more year to live. I didn't know that then, but I see how I had been prepared and equipped for what was just ahead. The 40-day personal journal area at the back of the book is a place to write and document prayers, thoughts, and lessons as the 40-day journey unfolds. In reviewing this book to recommend and reading over each day's call-out to God, I'm touched to see the grace and strength I was given during that season to endure.

GRIEF BOOKS FOR KIDS

My daughter has a doctorate in Counseling, in addition to teaching for a Masters in Counseling program, and has a certificate in Play Therapy. She has suggested the following books for kids who are grieving.

Grief has long arms and touches the lives of everyone, no matter how old or small. If you have a child in your circle of grief, here are her recommendations. I now have them in my library, too. These books have become an important addition to keep and even read for myself. Their message for those who grieve doesn't change with age.

- *Tear Soup, A Recipe for Healing After Loss* by Pat Schwiebert and Chuck DeKlyen (ISBN 0-9615197-6-2) The cover of this book explains that it is a read for all ages. I completely agree. The beautiful illustrations mark this as a children's book, but the message in the text is for every age. The story is compelling, tender, and powerful. The main character, Grandy, has suffered a major loss and uses making a pot of Tear Soup as a way to describe and process her grief. Children will be drawn into the story as easily as adults. I was very touched by reading Tear Soup and even had a few tears fill my own eyes reading it. This is a highly recommended book for children, but adults will be affirmed in their grief as well.

- *The Memory Box: A Book About Grief* by Joanna Rowland (ISBN 978-1-5064-2672-3) This book has been given the Mom's Choice Award Honoring Excellence, The Midwest Book Award Finalist Medal, and the Moonbeam Children's Book Award. The story is simple, the text is easy to read, and the message is very powerful. A striking story of loss poses questions in the text that children will ask in their grief, such as, "What happens to your love now that you are gone? Did it die too?" This book addresses big questions that grief presses into little hearts in beautifully simple, true words. The book is written from the perspective of a young child, but all ages will be touched by the easy way it supports the reader to start talking about their loss. This is a book I will keep on my shelf as a great resource for loss at any age.

- *The Memory Book Journal: A Grief Journal for Children and Families* by Joanna Rowland (ISBN 978-1-5064-5781-9) This book is designed as a journal to write in and a keepsake to remember the person who has died. It allows families to work together in writing, drawing, gluing, or taping memories of the one who has passed. This book journal is designed to be an ongoing process as anniversaries, holidays, or special events occur. It becomes a place where memories can be stored. The prompts are fluid enough to allow for any age or creative expression. It's a wonderful way for families to process grief together. This book is the companion to *The Memory Box: A Book about Grief* by the same author. That story is about creating a box of memories to remember the one who has died. The journal book pairs perfectly as the place to do just that. *The Memory Book Journal* encourages kids to have a place to keep their memories of their loved ones, a good way to help process grief.

- *Someone I Loved Died* By Christine Harder Tangvald, (ISBN 978-0-8307-7555-2) This book is for kids. The text is especially geared towards the thoughts and questions filling a child's mind concerning death. In an understanding way, the author addresses fears, loss, and heaven in terms a child would relate to. There is space to draw feelings and pictures. There are questions to answer concerning the death of the person who has died. I like this book's straightforward approach to help kids understand death, giving them words to express what is so hard to come to terms with at any age. Heaven is addressed as a real place, and there is a faith-based approach to discussing it. The book's last page is a helpful guide for parents or adults on how to support a child facing grief.

- *God I Need to Talk to You about Feeling Sad* by Susan K. Leigh (ISBN 978-0-7586-3434-4) This small book of only seven pages, measuring 4 inches, is just kid-size. The illustrations have a kid appeal, and the text is written from a child's point of view. The short story deals with sadness from loss and gives the okay for tears while assuring God understands even when we are sad—a good reminder for us all.

- *The Invisible String* by Patrice Karst, (ISBN 13978-0-316-48623-1) This children's book has a universal message. The story opens up to a child that no matter what happens or what they are afraid of, an invisible string ties them to the people who love them. They are never alone. This book is a comfort at a time when grief can cause a child to feel very disconnected and not understand why. It is not necessarily a book about childhood grief; however, the comfort and security it describes would be very helpful and consoling during a difficult time.

MORE RECIPES

Adding recipes and recommended cookbooks to a grief book might seem odd, but cooking and sharing food has become a way that I now share community and friendship, especially now that I'm filing taxes as "single."

You may not be so inclined to spend time in the kitchen, but that's okay. Take-out is a lovely way to share food, throw a party, invite a friend over, or celebrate an occasion, even with just yourself.

In this section, you'll find a few recommended cookbooks and more of my favorite go-to recipes:

- Homemade Applesauce
- Baked Apples
- Really Easy Tomato Soup
- Carol's Whack-Biscuit Chicken Casserole
- Cathy's Stuffed Mushrooms
- Super Easy Pot Pie
- Super Meatloaf
- Lori's Angel Hair Baked Spaghetti
- Jeanette's Fabulous Frosted Brownies

- Fresh Strawberry Cream Pie
- Better Than Store-Bought Chocolate Sauce
- Crock Pot Pork Chops
- Slow Cooker Pulled Pork with…
- Homemade BBQ Sauce
- Slaw
- Prosciutto-Wrapped Asparagus
- Salmon Three Ways

My intention with adding recipes isn't to create a cookbook; it's to remind you that you're not alone in your grief. Comfort appears in many other forms; food is another expression of comfort I enjoy sharing.

I may have gone to culinary school, but there are still days when dinner is a bowl of cereal eaten while standing at the kitchen counter. My journey through grief has taught me that easy, tasty, accessible recipes I've already shared and the ones below can lift spirits more than a bowl of cereal.

Enjoy!

~ Janet

HOMEMADE APPLESAUCE

Homemade apple sauce is one of the easiest ways to fill your kitchen with warm, cozy goodness. I don't like soft apples. For some reason, I always buy a big bag of crunchy goodness and never seem to get them all eaten before they become too soft to eat and reject.

What should I do? Make applesauce!

This is one of those recipes with no specific measurements, just basic ingredients, and nothing can go wrong. It's very forgiving and easy, perfect for days you need such things.

Ingredients:

- Apples peeled or not
- Sugar, to your taste
- Salt, just a pinch
- Cinnamon

Peeling the apples is up to you. If you don't, the sauce must go through a sieve when cooking is finished to remove the peel. So the choice is up to you.

Directions:

1. Wash the apples (peel or not) and cut into 4ths. Remove the core and seeds.
2. Place cut apples into a heavy pot and add water to almost cover them. Don't drown them; not all the pieces need to be submerged.
3. Heat the pot on low until the water slowly simmers. Soon, the apples will get softer and softer. I like to squish them down as this happens to help with the sauciness. You can leave some chunks if you want a more chunky sauce.
4. Add some sugar here. Start with about ¼ cup at a time, and give a sprinkle of cinnamon. This is a tasting recipe. Taste as the apples get more and more cooked to get the sweetness and cinnamon just right. Add more sugar or cinnamon to your preference while stirring.
5. Keep stirring slowly. The applesauce will get thicker and thicker as the water evaporates, the apples cook down, and the sugar takes over. The bubbles will be thick, so stirring here is important to get the texture right and not burn the bottom.
6. When the apple sauce looks and tastes how you want, it's sweet and full of enough cinnamon. Add a pinch of salt and let the mixture cool.

Your kitchen will smell like an apple pie, and you will love how easy it is to make a favorite comfort side dish. ENJOY!

BAKED APPLES

These baked apples are another option for apples that are too soft to eat. However, firm or sour apples are a perfect choice, too. This recipe will effortlessly make your kitchen burst with apple pie aroma.

If you're in the grocery store and want some specific ideas, these are good apples to keep an eye out for Granny Smith, Honey Crisp, Pink Lady, Gala, or any other style you happen to have.

Ingredients:

For 4 Baked Apples:

- ¼ cup brown sugar
- ¼ cup chopped walnuts, *optional*
- ¼ cup raisins, *optional*
- 1 teaspoon of cinnamon
- 1 tablespoon of butter
- ¾ cup boiling water
- Additional butter, as needed

If you are baking more (increase the ingredients) or fewer than four apples, decrease the ingredient amount.

Directions:

1. Set the oven to 375 degrees Fahrenheit.
2. Wash the apples and trim the bottoms to allow them to stand straighter in the baking dish. Otherwise, the sugary goodness will spill out during cooking, which would be a shame.
3. Transform the apple into a bowl. Core out the center of the apple to remove the core and the seeds. (This is the hardest part of the recipe!) Be careful not to cut through the bottom of the apple for the same reason stated above about sugary goodness.
4. With a paring knife, cut out the stem. Take a small spoon to well out enough room to allow packing brown sugar, raisins, and nuts. The opening should be an inch or so, depending on the apple size. Bore down, leave about ½ inch of the bottom of the apple intact.
5. Place the apples in a baking dish with sides.
6. Mix the sugar, cinnamon, *nuts, and raisins in a small bowl if using*. Pack this evenly into the apples. Top each apple with ¼ of the butter.
7. Place the apples into the baking dish and pour ¾ cup of boiling water into the dish.
8. Bake at 375 degrees until the apples are tender but not mushy, about 30–45 minutes. You can test the doneness by sticking a small knife into the top to test for softness.
9. When done, spoon to baste some of the juice from cooking over the hot apples. Serve with ice cream.

YUM! Comfort Goodness!

REALLY EASY TOMATO SOUP

You might think it's not worth it to make from scratch tomato soup, especially when there is perfectly good soup from a can or a carton. Trust me. It's worth the really easy effort.

The few ingredients for the soup's foundation can't be beat. It stands alone with yummy goodness. Screams for a grilled cheese sandwich pairing. (Try the Potato Chip Grilled Cheese recipe from Week 2, Day 7!)

Plus, this recipe has lots of room to add more to it.

Ingredients:

Makes 4 generous servings.

- 2 Large onions, chopped into large chunks
- One 28-oz can of whole tomatoes
- One 28-oz can tomato sauce (not spaghetti sauce)
- 8 Tablespoons of butter (1 stick)
- Handful of fresh basil leaves to add before blending (optional but suggested—fantastic!)
- Add 1–2 cups of chicken broth or water if soup gets too thick.

Directions:

1. Melt the butter in a heavy soup pot. When bubbly, toss in the chopped onion and sauté until just soft, only a few minutes.
2. Add tomato sauce and whole tomatoes; don't drain.
3. Sprinkle in 3/4 teaspoon salt.
4. Bring to a simmer, uncovered, for about 30–35 minutes.
5. Stir the mixture occasionally.
6. Add whole basil leaves if you are using them at this time.
7. With an Immersion blender, blend the soup into smooth loveliness to your liking. Keep some chunks of tomato or onion if you like. Or, if you don't have a hand-held blender, here are some *alternative blending methods:* Pour into a blender in batches (caution, it's hot!) Or use a hand-held potato masher until the soup becomes your preferred consistency.
8. Add seasoning to taste.

Additions to Consider:

- Stir in leftover rice to make Tomato Rice Soup.
- Add leftover cooked pasta or orzo for a nice texture.
- I've even thrown in leftover steamed veggies.
- Grated cheese on top or add croutons.

ENJOY!

CAROL'S WHACK-BISCUIT CHICKEN CASSEROLE

I MUST FIRST EXPLAIN WHAT "WACK-BISCUITS" are. I credit my brother Scott, who once asked our mom to make wack-biscuits, "the kind you wack on the edge of the counter to open the tube." Our family has named these easy-to-prepare buttermilk biscuits.

My sister, Carol, perfected this yummy, really easy chicken casserole, and she is legendary for fixing it for anyone who needs some casserole comfort—including our family recipe in this book only seemed right. I hope you give this one a try.

It pairs well with homemade applesauce.

Ingredients:

- 1 16-ounce tube of Pillsbury (or another brand of refrigerator biscuits in a "tube")
- 1 block of cream cheese
- 1 onion, diced
- 2 cups of cooked chicken: rotisserie works well, canned chicken works well, or leftover chicken works well, too.
- 1 can of cream chicken soup. (Cream of mushroom works well, and cream of celery works well, too.)

- 2 tablespoons butter
- Sautéed diced onion
- 1–2 cups shredded Cheese (Cheddar, Colby, Monetary, or any combo of cheeses)

Directions:

Remove the biscuit tube from the refrigerator for a few minutes to make spreading them in the pan easier.

1. Spray a 13x9-inch baking dish with cooking spray.
2. Melt butter and sauté diced onion until soft and translucent.
3. Open the tube of biscuits per instruction on the tube. (My childhood memory is a "whack" on the counter for opening. However, a spoon inserted into the seam of the biscuit roll works much better.)
4. Fill the bottom of the baking dish with the biscuit rounds. Press them down and stretch the dough to cover the dish. Pinch the individual biscuit seams together to combine all the biscuits into a slab of dough. Pulling and stretching won't affect the crust results.
5. Spread cooked onion onto the biscuit dough crust
6. Spread chicken to cover.
7. Break off pieces of cream cheese and dot to cover the chicken
8. In a separate bowl, mix the soup and some milk (measure half of the empty soup can) and mix the combination until smooth.
9. Pour the soup mixture to cover the ingredients.
10. Top with shredded cheese to cover.

Bake at 350 degrees for 30–35 minutes until hot and bubbly around the edges.

Let it sit for a few minutes.

CATHY'S STUFFED MUSHROOMS

I COULDN'T INCLUDE one sister's recipe without adding one from my other sister, Cathy. She and I have much in common; we married brothers and had a double wedding. Her stuffed mushroom recipe is so easy, a no-brainer to serve if friends drop by and you need a fabulously easy appetizer or just find yourself wanting a warm bite of yumminess—a must-try.

PS, Cathy hated mushrooms her whole life until she made this recipe!

Ingredients:

- 8 oz white mushroom, cleaned and stems removed. Depending on the mushroom size or the number of mushrooms you are stuffing, you may need to double the above ingredient amount.
- ½ cup Smoked Gouda cheese, shredded. (**Must** be the smoked Gouda)
- 1 tablespoon slivered almonds, toasted and chopped
- 1 tablespoon Mayonnaise

Directions:

1. Preheat the oven to 350 degrees.
2. Lightly dry the cleaned mushroom caps.
3. Grate the cheese into a small bowl.
4. Add the toasted almonds to the bowl and toss to combine.
5. Spoon in enough mayonnaise to bind the cheese and almonds.
6. Stuff each mushroom cap with enough cheese mixture to fill.
7. Place all filled mushroom caps with filling-side facing up onto a baking pan. (Optional: Line the baking pan with parchment paper.)
8. Bake at 350 degrees until the cheese is soft and melty, about 10 minutes, and the mushrooms seem soft but not mushy. (Note: Cooking time depends on the size of the mushrooms, so keep a careful eye on the oven.)

These quick, easy show-stopper stuffed mushrooms will be a must-make again once you sink your teeth into just one!

TA-DAH!

SUPER EASY POT PIE

NOT MUCH SAYS comfort like a homemade pot pie. This is one of the easiest pot pies to make, full of vegetables and creamy filling. No one will know it's made from such easy ingredients. Tastes great.

Ingredients:

- 2 cans of Veg-All Mixed Vegetables. (I'm not a fan of canned veggies, except for the brand in this recipe—It's good) Or 12 oz of thawed frozen mixed vegetables.
- 1 can cream of chicken soup or mushroom soup
- Half a soup can of milk
- 1 small onion, diced and sautéd
- 1 Tablespoon butter
- 1 package of Pillsbury pre-made pie crust, two crusts, room temperature.
- 2–3 cups cooked chicken. Rotisserie, leftover, or a large can of chicken.

Directions:

1. In a large bowl, mix sautéd onion, chicken, and vegetables. Mix the milk with the soup in a small bowl and add to the chicken mixture. Toss to combine.
2. Line a 9-inch pie plate with the first crust. Mound the filling into the crust. Top with the second crust and crimp the edges to seal both crusts and flute. Make a few slits at the top of the pie for steam to escape.
3. Bake at 400 degrees for 35 minutes or until browned and bubbly. If the edges of the pie brown too quickly before its finish, use strips of aluminum foil to cover the edges.

That's it! This easy pot pie is a delicious comfort.

SUPER MEATLOAF

I'M SHARING a cooking secret that I've never bragged about. I get rave reviews when I make a meatloaf, but I have never given the recipe until now. It's because I cheat. It's not like looking at someone's test paper, which is kind of cheating, but I use a meatloaf packaged spice mix. As a culinary person, I try to make food from scratch, but this meatloaf preparation is so good and foolproof.

Ingredients:

- 1 McCormick Meatloaf Spice Packet or your grocery brand Meatloaf Spice Packet.
- 2 pounds of lean ground beef
- 2 eggs
- Some milk
- Bread crumbs or bread crumbled
- Prepare the meat as directed on the spice package.

Directions:

1. Follow the specific directions on the McCormick Meatloaf Spice Packet. (Or the spice packet you are using.

2. Shape into a loaf.
3. Bake as directed.

The house smells fantastic, and you've got yourself a plate of comfort food to rave about.

LORI'S ANGEL HAIR SPAGHETTI PIE

HAVE you ever been in the mood for spaghetti but needed something more? This recipe is just the ticket. My sister-in-law, Lori, serves this as a family favorite. It always brings their son, Jackson, home for dinner. I like to serve it with a simple salad and Italian bread, especially if the bread is doctored up a bit. (See at the end of the recipe for my way of preparing.)

Ingredients:

- 6 ounces of cooked Angel Hair Pasta
- 2 Tablespoons butter
- 2 eggs, well-beaten
- ⅓ cup Parmesan cheese
- 1 pound of ground beef
- 1 onion chopped
- 1 cup of cottage cheese
- 1 cup of mozzarella cheese, shredded
- Jar Pasta Sauce (Rao's Marina is superb)

Directions:

1. Cook pasta as directed, and drain.
2. Mix into the spaghetti, butter, beaten eggs, and Parmesan cheese.
3. Place the mixture into a 9-inch buttered pie plate, spreading to cover.
4. Brown the ground beef with the chopped onion. Crumble the meat as it cooks. Drain any fat.
5. Add the pasta sauce to the meat mixture.
6. Spread cottage cheese over the pasta layer. Next, spread the meat sauce over the cottage cheese layer.
7. Bake at 350 degrees for 40 minutes. Top with shredded mozzarella cheese and bake 5 minutes longer until the cheese is melty.
8. Let the Spaghetti rest for about 5 minutes and cut it into wedges.

Yummy!

It pairs well with a nice simple salad and a homemade classic Dijon Vinaigrette dressing. See Week 3, Day 21 for the super easy recipe.

I like to cut Italian bread into chunks, brush each side with olive oil, not forgetting a few turners of coarse sea salt, and bake until warm, crunchy, and a little salty. Awesome.

JEANETTE'S FABULOUS FROSTED BROWNIES

These brownies are requested at every family gathering, hands down. My other sister-in-law is so famous for these gems, among the family, it's simply known as Jeanette's Brownies. No more need be said.

This fabulous chocolate melt-in-your-mouth brownie will also become a favorite in your circle! The best part is that you won't believe how simple the recipe is. That's why she calls it "No recipe brownies."

Ingredients:

- 2 boxes of your favorite dark chocolate fudge brownie mix and the ingredients per package instructions.
- 1 can of your favorite Classic Vanilla icing.
- 1 oz Baker's unsweetened chocolate, melted. (It must be the unsweetened chocolate.)
- *Optional: Add crushed or chopped nuts*

Directions:

1. Prepare brownies as the package directs, doubling ingredients

because you are using two boxes of brownie mix. *(Optional: Add nuts to the batter)*
2. Pour into a 13x9 glass baking dish, sprayed with cooking spray.
3. Bake as the package directs, however…
4. **The key here is to under-bake the brownies slightly so they are chewy. Cool in the pan.**
5. Spread vanilla icing over the cooled brownies. Drizzle the melted chocolate square over the icing. Use a flat knife to spread gently and evenly over the top of the vanilla icing. *(Optional: Sprinkle chopped nuts onto the top!)*

That's all, folks! The legend of brownies is now yours!

FRESH STRAWBERRY CREAM PIE

OH BOY! It is always the reaction to this really easy pie. My sister makes it often, and we're always happy when she does. You'll love how easy and pretty this pie looks, but it doesn't last long; there are never leftovers.

Ingredients:

- 1 quart of strawberries left whole.
- 1 8 oz package cream cheese, softened
- ½ cup granulated sugar
- ¼-½ teaspoon of Almond extract
- 8 oz Cool Whip, thawed
- Slivered toasted almonds, if desired
- 1 ready-to-fill, 9-inch graham cracker crust
- Chocolate Sauce to drizzle on top (See next recipe for homemade chocolate sauce!)

Directions:

1. Wash and hull strawberries. Keep whole. Trim the bottom so they stand upright.

2. Cream the cream cheese, sugar, and almond extract with an electric mixer until smooth.
3. Fold in thawed Cool Whip
4. Pour mixture into prepared graham cracker crust
5. Sprinkle toasted almonds across the top of the pie
6. Chill at least 1 hour
7. Before serving, add completely dry whole strawberries pointed side up around the top of the pie.
8. Drizzle with chocolate sauce. See below for an easy chocolate sauce recipe, or purchased sauce works well, too.

BETTER THAN STORE BOUGHT CHOCOLATE SAUCE

After I made homemade chocolate sauce for friends coming for dinner, I decided never to use store-bought again! It's so easy and so much better.

Ingredients:

- ½ cup unsweetened cocoa powder (I like Ghirardelli)
- ¾ cup sugar
- 1 ¼ cups milk (whole milk, 2% or half-and-half)
- 1 ½ Tablespoons flour (to thicken)
- 2 Tablespoons butter
- A Pinch of salt
- ¾-1 Teaspoon vanilla to add when cooking is completed

Directions:

1. Mix the cocoa powder and flour until well combined. Heat the milk on medium-low heat. Stir in the butter until it melts.
2. Increase heat to medium-high
3. Stir the cocoa powder mixture slowly into the warm milk.

4. Keep stirring for 5 or 6 minutes as the sauce simmers.
5. Add the vanilla and a pinch of salt.

This sauce stays "pourable" even when stored in the refrigerator, so it is ready whenever a bowl of ice cream calls.

CROCK POT PORK CHOPS

I'VE BEEN a crock pot lover for decades. I don't know who the inventor was, but bless them! I'm sure they had a large, hungry family and were busy all day.

Anyone who wants to eat when they walk in the door is the audience for using a slow cooker. There are thousands of recipes; this is one of my go-to when I want super easy comfort and remember to assemble in the morning!

Ingredients:

- Any kind of pork chop, but thicker bone works best
- Any number of chops (6-8 works well for my 7-quart slow cooker.)
- 1–2 onions, sliced into rings
- 1 can of Cream of mushroom soup
- 1 can of cream of something else soup, chicken, celery, or another can of mushroom soup
- A bit more than half a soup can of water, chicken broth, or even apple juice is particularly tasty.

- If so inclined, I've even sliced up an apple and added it with the onion layer for flavor.
- You can add mushrooms, whole or sliced.

Directions:

1. Lightly brown the pork chops in olive oil or butter for a nice browned appearance.
2. While browning, season with salt and pepper or any favorite spice blend. I particularly like Trader Joe's 21 Seasoning Salute Spice Blend.
3. Line the bottom of the cooker with the sliced onion rings and place the chops on top. Layer the meat to fit the cooker. I like to add onion slices in between layers to add flavor. Add mushrooms if using.
4. In a small bowl, mix the liquid with the soup. Blend well and pour over the pork chops. Put the lid on, and Ta-Dah! Dinner is made.
5. Cook on low for 6-8 hours. A low setting is best for moist chops.
6. The gravy that the pork chops and soups produce can be thickened by mixing 1 tablespoon of cornstarch and 1 tablespoon of cold water. Add the paste to the cooker and stir in. Give it about 5 minutes. You can add more additions to this thickening agent to get the thickness that looks right to you. That's it.

It pairs well with cooked noodles and rice and is really great with mashed potatoes.

SLOW COOKER PULLED PORK

HERE'S a recipe I've made for decades. Having roots in the South and loving sloppy meaty sandwiches, especially topped with drippy slaw, this recipe has served me well. It feeds a crowd and is so easy to make.

The cut of pork used here matters. A pork shoulder or pork butt roast works best, as the fat content makes for meat so tender it practically shreds itself.

Ingredients:

- 3-4 pound pork shoulder roast or pork butt roast, season well on all sides with salt and pepper and spice blend mix if you like
- 1-2-onions sliced
- ½ cup cooking liquid (water, stock. Apple juice, or beer)

Directions:

1. Set the temp to LOW for 8–10 hours.
2. When the cooking is complete, carefully remove the meat from a cutting board. I like to pick through and remove any fatty

pieces. It will fall apart tender here and be easy to shred, but to completely shred, return it to the cooker.
3. Use two forks to shred the pork into barbecue sandwich-size shreds.
4. Dump the cooking liquid to prevent diluting the barbeque sauce later.
5. Return the shredded meat to the slow cooker.
6. Add *Super Good BBQ Sauce* or your favorite BBQ sauce to taste
7. Turn the crockpot to its warm setting
8. Serve pulled pork on hamburger buns (tastes great with the *Slaw* recipe too!)

SUPER GOOD BBQ SAUCE

ADD this to the Slow Cooker Pulled Pork for a yummy pairing and some good eating! It's great leftover, too, if there is any!

Ingredients:

- 1 cup maple syrup (I like to use pure maple syrup)
- 1 cup ketchup

Directions:

1. Mix your ingredients.
2. Heat on the stove.
3. It's truly that easy and so yummy!

SLAW

Here in the South, coleslaw is just known as Slaw. It tops hot dogs, sits next to fried fish and hush puppies, and is a crowning touch atop a pulled pork sandwich dripping with BBQ sauce. I love making the dressing from scratch, even though there are decent prepared bottles at the grocery. So, no shame if that's the route you take. However, this recipe is easy and good!

I've used a bag of prepared shredded coleslaw cabbage, that's fine, or shred the cabbage yourself using a sharp knife or a large hole cheese grater. Add grated carrots for a little color if you like. But just straight cabbage is fine.

Ingredients:

- ¾ c - 1 cup mayonnaise
- A splash of apple cider vinegar
- A teaspoon or more of sugar
- Salt and pepper to taste.

Directions:

1. In a small bowl, mix until smooth the above ingredients.
2. This is a taste-as-you-go recipe. If you like it a little sweeter, add more sugar. If it needs more tang, add a teaspoon or more vinegar.
3. Once to your liking, pour the dressing over the cabbage in a large bowl and mix thoroughly.

That's it. Slaw is ready to sit atop your BBQ or as a side to anything yummy.

PROSCIUTTO WRAPPED ASPARAGUS

HERE'S another super easy appetizer that will impress the socks off anyone you serve it to, including yourself. I've served this for a silent auction dinner party I catered that went for $3,000 (along with the earlier stuffed mushrooms recipe), and they couldn't get enough. Two ingredients, as the title says, and that's it.

Ingredients:

- Sheets of Prosciutto, one for each asparagus.
- Asparagus, thick spears work best, but thin ones are fine. Really thin sizes can be bundled together.

Directions:

1. Trim the fresh asparagus to remove the woody-looking stem end.
2. Wrap each spear of asparagus in a thin sheet of prosciutto from the bottom to the top. It will look a bit like a stripe on a candy cane. If the prosciutto is thinly cut, it may tear and look messy on the wrap; just press the rips into the twist and keep

going. The trick is to start at the bottom of the stalk and wrap upwards.
3. Repeat until the desired number of asparagus are wrapped.
4. Place the prepared asparagus on a cookie sheet. Line the cookie sheet with parchment paper if you like, but this is not necessary (easier clean up).
5. Bake at 425 degrees until the prosciutto is crispy and the asparagus feels slightly limp, firm, but tender. I stick a sharp knife into a spear to test.
6. Cook for 10 minutes or more; cooking time depends on your oven and the thickness of the spheres.
7. Let them cool for a minute and serve on a platter. They make the perfect finger food for any occasion.

CHRIS'S FRESH SALMON THREE WAYS

I couldn't miss including one of my favorite son-in-law's recipes. The recipe is a favorite, and so is the son-in-law!! Salmon is a staple in their house, and it's always a treat for me when he makes salmon cakes. He's a natural in the kitchen and enjoys being the chef of his family. Here are his three ways to prepare salmon. He doesn't use recipes, so the directions give you room to use your judgment. Don't worry; salmon is easy to cook and even better to eat.

CHRIS' BAKED SALMON

Basic Ingredients:

- 1-1.5 inch salmon filet
- Lemon
- Salt and pepper
- Onion powder

Directions:

1. Preheat oven to 400 degrees.

2. Season fish: Squeeze lemon juice onto the fish. Sprinkle it with salt and pepper and garlic powder.
3. Bake for 18 minutes. Enjoy or use it to make the salmon cakes.

CHRIS' PAN FRIED SALMON

Basic Ingredients:

- 1-1.5 inch salmon filet
- Lemon
- Salt and pepper
- Onion powder

Directions:

1. Prepare the salmon filet: gently wash the fish in cold water, then pat dry it with paper towels.
2. Season: Apply salt and pepper, garlic powder, and onion powder.
3. Preheat a cast iron skillet on medium-high heat. Add enough cooking oil to coat the pan. Once the oil is shimmering and slightly smoking, gently lay the salmon skin side up and cook for 3 minutes or until it separates from the pan without effort, then flip. Once flipped, carefully add lemon juice to the fish and cook for another 3-4 minutes or until the salmon separates. Enjoy.

CHRIS' SALMON CAKES

Basic Ingredients:

- 1-1.5 inch salmon filet
- Lemon
- Salt and pepper
- Onion powder

Additional ingredients:

- 1 small diced bell pepper
- 1 diced onion
- 2 Eggs
- Bread Crumbs to bind
- Mayo to bind
- Worcestershire Sauce

Directions:

1. Bake the salmon using the above Baked Salmon recipe.
2. In a saute pan, cook the onions and bell peppers in a few tablespoons of cooking oil and saute until the onion is translucent and the peppers are slightly soft. Take off the heat to cool.
3. Flake the cooked salmon in a medium bowl with the onion, peppers, mayo, Worcestershire sauce, and eggs. Add breadcrumbs, mixing until the mixture doesn't stick to your hands. Ball up the mixture into 2-inch balls and flatten to about ½ inch thickness.
4. Preheat the cast iron skillet to medium-high heat and coat with cooking oil. Fry the salmon cakes on each side for 3-5 minutes until a nice brown crust appears. Ta-Dah! Enjoy.

ACKNOWLEDGMENTS

There are people who enter your life, who have the special ability to give your life story the wings it needs for it to be told and the courage to tell it. Emily Ann Peterson is that one for me. She has come alongside on the journey of this book and managed to maneuver through the rough seas of editing, encouraging and taking on the challenge of not letting me quit.

Finding the Meaning of Grief needed the support and loving care of a dedicated professional to tie up the loose ends, rearrange chapters, propose questions, ask for more detail and be willing to read the document hundreds of times. I'm so thankful for the care Emily Ann showed me and the words written in this book to help make it a read to help heal your heart and hopefully give you courage to tell your story too.

Thank you Emily Ann Peterson.

ABOUT THE AUTHOR

If you live long enough, grief and heartache will find you. The broken heart is part of our human story. It can define us, break us, or make us stronger. That is the tale of Janet Haney's first book, *Hello Nobody: Standing at The Door Alone, What To Do When Everything Changes*. Janet's son died at age nine. Her husband battled prostate cancer for many years and lost the fight. She fought breast cancer alone. Everything had changed, and suddenly, she found herself walking into an empty house. It was then that she knew it was time to tell her story.

Write Your Way Through Change: a 21-Day Devotional for Grief & Major Life Transitions is Haney's gift to her readers after she experienced such healing from writing her own story with page and pen. Each day holds a note of encouragement and writing prompts for further exploration.

Haney brings a healing balm of camaraderie to the heartache of every reader. Her grief is not tied with a neat and tidy bow, neither is yours. Attending her workshops and lectures and reading her books will give you someone to stand alongside who has discovered that courage comes while walking the trail set before us.

She lives in Kentucky, splitting her time visiting family across the country. Her grandchildren are her new joy.

Join her community at **jhaney.com**

ALSO BY JANET HANEY

Hello Nobody: Standing at the Door Alone-What to Do When Everything Changes

Write Your Way Through Change: a 21-Day Devotional Journal for Grief & Major Life Transitions

Finding the Meaning of Grief: 6 Weeks of Devotionals for Exploring Comfort & Hope

www.ingramcontent.com/pod-product-compliance
Lightning Source LLC
Chambersburg PA
CBHW030431010526
44118CB00011B/589